AURORA VEY

Subtle Reflections

For my children, the reason I kept fighting. And for myself, the proof that I could.

From every wound there is a scar, and every scar tells a story. A story that says, 'I survived.'

- Craig Scott

Contents

Preface

I never imagined I would write these pages. For years, I carried my story in silence — the weight of trauma, the echoes of broken promises, the scars that refused to fade. I told myself it was easier to bury the pain than to face it. But silence has a way of suffocating, and the truth has a way of demanding to be heard. This memoir is not about perfection. It is about survival.

I write these words not to relive the hurt, but to release it. To air out the dirty laundry so I can breathe again. To show that healing is not linear, forgiveness is not simple, and strength is not born from ease but from endurance.

If pieces of your story echo in mine, know that you are not alone. We are imperfect, but we are resilient, and that resilience is enough

Acknowledgments

This book is stitched together not only from my own survival, but from the people who stood beside me, shaped me, and reminded me that even in the darkest moments, I was never truly alone.

To my daughter — You are the light that kept me moving when everything felt too heavy to hold. In these pages, you'll see pieces of the weight I carried, but know this: every step forward, every breath I fought for, was for you. You gave me laughter on days I didn't think I had any left, and hope when hope felt impossible. This book belongs to you as much as it does to me.

To my son — You are the reason I kept breathing when the world felt too dark. As you read these pages, you'll see the battles I walked through, but remember this: every moment of strength I found, I found because of you. You brought joy into places that had forgotten it, and you reminded me that love can pull us through anything. This book is yours just as much as it is mine.

To my neighbor — im glad I didnt call AAA. though your name is left unchanged, we all know who *THE* neighbor is. You've been the one steady presence through my chaos, the witness to my breakdowns, and the one who never turned away. Thank you for being the kind of neighbor who became family. You'll get the first copy of this book — redacted like a government file, but signed with my name. Proof that you survived living next door to me, which is no small feat.

To Jessie — thank you for being the kind of friend who showed up with honesty, humor, and zero hesitation. You never sugarcoated anything, you never disappeared when things got messy, and you always knew how to pull me back to myself when I was spiraling. I'm grateful for every laugh, every late-night talk, and every moment you reminded me I wasn't alone.

To my mom — I didn't write much about us here, but I want you to know I love you. Thank you for always trying your best, both as a mother and as a grandmother. Even when life made it hard, your effort was still love, and I carry that with me.

To my niece — you are my favorite niece, and I look forward to our morning calls when you read this book. I can't wait to laugh, cry, and talk through these pages with you. You remind me that joy and connection are still possible, even after everything.

To Poppop — though you are no longer here, your presence is still felt in every step I take. You taught me resilience, patience, and the quiet strength of family. Even in your absence, I carry your lessons with me, and I hope this book honors the love you gave. This is as much a tribute to your memory as it is to my survival.

and To Matthew — you may never get to read these words, but I hope you heal too. I hope you know I will never love anyone the way I loved you. You were my comfort and my chaos, my coffee and my tea, but also my pain. You left a mark that shaped me, and this book carries pieces of that story too. I don't know what the future will hold, but I know I have to keep going — for us.

And to everyone else who carried me in ways big and small —

thank you. This memoir is as much yours as it is mine.

1

Fractured Beginnings

The air was heavy, and I carried it in my chest—the weight of everything I couldn't say out loud. Smiles came easy enough when people were watching, but behind closed doors the cracks showed. I was tired, worn down, fractured in ways no one could see.

I grew up in survival mode. We lived in a small apartment on the east side of Providence. The floors were carpeted throughout, except for the kitchen, where the linoleum was worn and peeling at the edges. The walls carried the faint smell of old cooking and cigarette smoke that seemed to seep in from the neighbors. It was cramped, every sound carried through, and privacy was almost impossible.

At night, I would find my mother at the kitchen table. She sat hunched over, her hair pulled back in a messy knot, her shoulders heavy with exhaustion. Her fingers gripped a pen like it was the only weapon she had.

The lamp on the table threw a weak yellow glow across the stacks of bills, highlighting the red stamps that screamed *past due*. The fridge hummed in the background, filling the silence between her sighs.

I stood in the doorway, barefoot, clutching the hem of my shirt. I wanted to ask if we were okay, if she was okay, but the words stuck in my throat. She looked up, her eyes tired but sharp. "Go back to bed, Aurora," she whispered, her voice soft but edged with warning.

"I can help," I said, my voice small, almost breaking.

She shook her head, forcing a smile that didn't reach her eyes. "We'll figure it out."

But even then, I knew better. Words didn't fix empty wallets. Promises didn't pay rent. I went back to bed, but sleep never came. I lay awake listening to the scratch of her pen, the shuffle of papers, the quiet sob she thought I couldn't hear.

The mornings after weren't much easier. I'd wake to the smell of burnt toast and the sound of her moving quickly, already dressed for work, already exhausted. She'd hand me a plate, kiss the top of mine and my sister Alyssa's head, and rush out the door. I ate alone, staring at the crumbs, wondering how long she could keep this up.

Later, when I made the dumb choice to move into Dad's house, I learned a different kind of survival. His place was a four-bedroom, two-story home in Glocester, Rhode Island, built back in the 1800s. It carried the weight of history in its bones— the kind of house where the past lingered in every creak of the floorboards and draft through the windows.

When he first got the house, the kitchen didn't even have floors—just dirt packed down from years of wear. Before we laid anything new, we dug into the ground to rebuild, and that's when the past revealed itself. Buried beneath the earth we found a cannonball, heavy and cold in our hands, its surface rough with age. Digging further into the rooms beside the kitchen, we uncovered one of those old bathrooms once built for slaves—crude, unsettling, a reminder of the history the house carried long before us.

The house felt haunted by more than just our secrets—it was haunted by the echoes of a nation divided, by the cruelty that had once been ordinary, by the weight of lives lived long before ours.

The walls were thin enough to hear everything, but thick enough to keep secrets trapped. I learned how to read silence, how to measure the tension in a room by the way people avoided each other's eyes. I remember standing in the hallway, listening to muffled voices behind closed doors. Lies layered on top of lies, until truth was slippery, impossible to hold. That house wasn't just old—it was built on history, treachery, and silence, and all of it pressed down on me until survival became the only way to live.

I learned to keep my own secrets too. To smile when people asked how things were, to nod when teachers said I looked tired, to pretend that someone I was supposed to trust hadn't just crawled into my bed again while my dad and the rest of the house slept soundly. That house taught me that silence could be louder than words, that sometimes the things unsaid carried more weight than anything spoken.

But silence didn't stay contained within those walls. It followed me as I moved from place to place, carrying the weight of instability like a shadow.

I feared the mornings too, when I had to put on the mask again, smiling at teachers, pretending to be fine. I carried the weight of deception, of instability, of secrets too heavy for a child to hold. After Dad's, I went back to Mom's for a while, only to end up briefly living at a friend's house. Rent there

3

wasn't paid in money—it was paid in booze. Her mother was an alcoholic, but she was kind enough to let me stay for a while.

And it didn't stop there. I went back to Dad's, then to Mom's, then to my aunt's. Each move was another fracture, another reminder that stability was something other people had. My aunt's house was crowded, full of voices and rules, but it was still temporary. Every new set of walls carried its own secrets, its own silences.

Eventually, I found myself at my Poppop's computer store, then living above a bar. The smell of stale beer drifted up through the floorboards, mixing with the hum of machines and the faint glow of neon signs outside. Nights were loud, filled with voices and music from below, but inside I felt the same familiar quiet—the kind of quiet that presses down on you, reminding you of everything you're trying not to feel.

Through all of it, I endured pain, fear, and the constant ache of uncertainty. I feared the nights most, when memories crept in and silence became unbearable.

Years later, months leading up to my first birth were a blur of fear and exhaustion. My body changed faster than my mind could catch up. I remember standing in front of the mirror, staring at the curve of my stomach, tracing it with my hand, whispering to myself that I was too young, too unprepared, too lost. People stared at me in grocery stores, their eyes lingering just long enough to remind me I was different. Some smiled politely, others frowned, and a few whispered behind my back. I learned to keep my chin up, even when shame pressed down on me like a weight.

Doctor's appointments became a rhythm. The sterile smell of the clinic, the cold stethoscope against my skin, the nurse's questions that felt more like judgments. "Do you have support at home?" she asked once, her pen hovering over the clipboard. I nodded, though the truth was complicated. Support was a word that felt flimsy, like a chair with one broken leg.

The night labor started, the world tilted. Pain ripped through me in waves, sharp and relentless. I remember clutching the edge of the hospital bed, sweat dripping down my forehead, my breath coming in short, gasps. Nurses moved quickly around me, their voices calm but urgent. "You're doing fine," one said, though I didn't believe her.

Hours turned into days blurred together. The fluorescent lights buzzed overhead, the monitor beeped steadily, and I felt like I was floating outside my own body. And then, suddenly, I was rushed for an emergency C-section and it was over. A cry pierced the room, high and desperate, and they placed her in my arms. Her skin was soft, her eyes squeezed shut, her tiny fists curling and uncurling. I stared at her, my heart pounding, my mind racing. In that moment, I wasn't a child anymore. I was a mother. Then I passed out.

The first night home was chaos. The crib wasn't ready, my milk supply hadn't come in, the bottles weren't lined up, and I was terrified of doing everything wrong. I sat on the floor with her in my arms, the room dim, the shadows long, whispering promises I wasn't sure I could keep. "I'll protect you," I said, my voice shaking. "I'll figure it out."

Motherhood changed me, but it didn't save me. It just meant I had to fight harder, hustle faster, reinvent myself again and again. I had more children, got married, and tried to build a family out of the fragments of my past. For a while, I believed in the promise of stability. But marriage brought its own battles, and eventually, divorce carved another scar into my story—one that unfolded while I was already trying to hold myself together in a new job.

Pharmaceuticals became the chapter in between, a place where I thought I could rebuild. The office smelled faintly of toner and burnt coffee, a mix that clung to the air no matter how many times the janitors sprayed the hallways with lemon cleaner. I remember the first time I walked in, clutching a new employee badge, my palms sweating as I swiped it across the scanner. The green light blinked, the door clicked open, and I thought: *This is it. This is stability.*

But beneath the surface, cracks formed. I felt them in the way managers avoided eye contact, in the way conversations stopped when I entered the room. I told myself I was imagining it, that paranoia was just exhaustion. Until the day they called me in.

The HR office was colder than the rest of the building. The blinds were drawn, the fluorescent light buzzing overhead. The manager sat across from me, her hands folded neatly on the desk. She spoke slowly, carefully, as if rehearsed. "We've decided to let you go. Get your stuff—you have two minutes."

The words hung in the air, heavy and final. My ears rang, my chest tightened, and I nodded like I understood, like I agreed. I didn't. I walked out into the parking lot, the sun too bright, the air too sharp, and sat in my car until the tears came.

I told myself I'd bounce back. I told myself it was just a setback. And for a while, I believed it. I found another position, another desk, another badge to swipe. I tried again.

But the second time, the betrayal cut deeper. Another cold office, another manager with rehearsed words. My hands shook as I signed the papers, but my jaw was set. This time, I didn't cry. I burned. I fought back. I filed a lawsuit, sat through hearings, listened to lawyers argue over my worth. And when the verdict came, I silently won.

Winning didn't feel like victory. It felt hollow, like standing in an empty room shouting into the void. The paycheck didn't erase the sleepless nights, the anxiety, the gnawing fear that I was disposable. It didn't erase the months of unemployment that followed, waking up every morning with dread pressing down on me like a weight I couldn't shake.

Unemployment was its own kind of prison. The silence of the phone, the rejection emails piling up, the way the days blurred together. I remember lying in bed, staring at the ceiling, listening to the sound of the world moving on without me. The mailbox became a place of dread. Thin envelopes with demanding words that all meant the same thing: *I owe someone money.* I stacked them on the counter until they became a tower, a monument to failure.

Days stretched into weeks while I was on unemployment. I tried to fill the hours—cleaning, cooking, pretending I had control—but the silence was louder than anything. I would sit by the window, watching cars pass, wondering how many of those drivers had jobs, how many of them felt secure. I envied strangers.

Sometimes I'd walk through the grocery store just to feel like part of the world again. I'd push the cart slowly, reading labels I couldn't afford, listening to the chatter of families around me. I'd linger in aisles, pretending to compare prices, just to stretch the time. The cashier would smile politely, ask if I found everything I needed, and I'd nod, even though what I needed couldn't be bought.

At night, the fear grew louder. I'd lie awake, staring at the ceiling, counting the cracks in the plaster, listening to the hum of the refrigerator. My kids would sleep in the next room, their breathing steady, their small bodies curled under their blankets. I'd whisper promises to them through the wall, promises I wasn't sure I could keep.

Later, after I found a new job, the days and nights carried a different kind of weight. During the day, I wore masks. At work, I smiled when colleagues passed by, laughed at jokes I didn't find funny, nodded through meetings while my mind screamed.

And now, here I am—on medical leave, with a new job that came after a long stretch of unemployment.

In grocery stores, I push the cart slowly, pretending to be just another mother buying milk and bread, while inside I'm calculating escape routes, scanning faces, bracing for danger that's not there.

This new job had arrived with promises of stability, of belonging, of a future I could finally trust. I wanted to believe those promises. But while working there, my marriage fractured. Divorce carved another scar into my story, leaving me to rebuild once again.

In the middle of that heartbreak, I opened my heart to someone new—a man I worked with. I thought love could heal me, that it could be the fresh start I deserved. Instead, it became another wound. What began as hope turned into disloyalty and abuse, a storm that followed me into the workplace and left me unable to step back into that office and face him.

The nights are still the worst. Sleep comes in fragments, broken by dreams that aren't dreams at all but memories replaying themselves in grotesque detail. I wake drenched in sweat, my heart pounding, my breath shallow, convinced for a moment that I was back there, trapped again. I sit up in bed, clutching the sheets, whispering to myself that I am safe, that it was over—even though my body refuses to believe it.

8

Trauma rewired me. It taught me to live in constant vigilance, to expect sellout, to anticipate pain.

I tried to explain it to friends, but words never seemed enough. How do you tell someone that your life is falling apart without sounding desperate? How do you explain that a door slamming can send your body into panic, or that the smell of cologne in a crowded elevator can make your knees buckle because it reminds you of him? Most friends would nod politely, their eyes darting away, uncomfortable with the weight of my truth. Others offered clichés—"time heals," "you're strong," "you'll get through this"—but time hasn't healed, strength isn't enough, and getting through it feels like dragging myself across broken glass.

Doctors tried to help. I sat in sterile offices, the walls painted in calming blues and greens, listening to professionals explain what I already knew: that my mind had been hijacked, that my body carried scars no one could see. They spoke in clinical terms—hypervigilance, flashbacks, dissociation—but those words felt too neat, too tidy, for the chaos inside me. PTSD wasn't just a diagnosis; it was a thief. It stole sleep, trust, joy, even the simple act of breathing without fear.

And yet, beneath all of it, there was a stubborn pulse. A refusal to disappear. Some nights, when the panic subsides, I like to sit by the window, watching the world outside. Streetlights glowed, cars passed, neighbors laughed on porches. Life went on, indifferent to my pain. And in those moments, I felt something small but undeniable: the urge to keep going. Not because I believed things would get better, but because I refused to let the world erase me.

That defiance became my anchor. Even when betrayal lingered and trauma refused to fade. Survival wasn't the same

9

as healing, but it was proof that I could keep moving. I am not whole, but I am still here—and sometimes, being here is enough.

Life has a way of carving us into shape through the places we've been and the people we've met. Each season leaves its mark, each chapter of living carries its own lessons. What came after was no different—moments that tested me, broke me, and built me all at once.

So while I'm not resting, I've been reflecting. It is the pause between battles, the moment when I look back at the child who grew up in survival mode, the young mother whispering promises in the dark, the wife who tried to hold a family together, the employee clutching a badge, desperate for stability, the woman sitting in HR offices, fighting back tears. All of those versions of me are still here, layered inside the person I am today.

The past is the past, but it is also the foundation of who I am. Each fraction of my life—every house, every stab in the back, every job lost, every relationship broken—shaped me. This book is about those fractions. Each chapter will go deeper into them, peeling back the layers of silence, survival, pretending, and resilience.

Right now, I am still in the middle of it. Medical leave is the space where I finally see the thread that connects it all. And that thread is me: scarred, exhausted, but still here. Still holding on to fragile hope. Still daring to believe in new promises.

2

House of Lies

I remember the night I pushed my sister Destiny out the window. Saying it now makes it sound brutal, but it wasn't violent. It was desperate, almost ritualistic—the kind of reckless act two kids invent when the walls feel too tight and the air too heavy. She wanted to run away from the horrors inside our home—the betrayals that lived in every corner, the secrets that poisoned the air—and she asked me to help her escape.

Destiny was only a little over a year older than me, but her scars ran deeper. I could see it in her eyes, the way they carried shadows even when she smiled. She had always been the one to lead me into rebellion—first the cigarette pressed between my lips, then the weed, and later other experimental drugs. She was fearless in ways I wasn't, and that fearlessness often pulled me along with her.

I remember the first time we did ecstasy together. Her room was dim, the posters curling at the edges, the old wooden floors worn thin from years of pacing. We sat cross-legged on the floor, beers sweating in our hands, the muffled sound of our parents drifting up from downstairs—laughter, clinking glasses, the hum of adult conversation that felt galaxies away from the world we were building upstairs.

The pill was small, almost innocent looking, but when I swallowed it with a gulp of beer, the world shifted. Colors sharpened about 40 minutes in, sounds stretched, the air itself seemed to hum. For a while, it felt like magic. But then the sickness came. It rose suddenly, a hot wave climbing from my stomach to my throat. I doubled over, panic flashing in my eyes.

Destiny didn't hesitate. She shoved an old boot into my hands, the leather cracked, the laces frayed. "Here," she said, her tone brisk, almost maternal. I bent over it, retching until the sour stench filled the room. The smell clung to the air, heavy and undeniable.

Footsteps creaked on the stairs. Our parents were coming up, their voices growing louder. Destiny's eyes widened, and for a moment we froze, caught between panic and defiance. She flicked off the lamp, shoved the boot under the bed, and hissed, "Lights out. Now."

The door opened, and our parents peeked in. "Everything okay?" one of them asked, scanning the room. We nodded, too quickly, our faces flushed. They lingered for a moment, suspicious, then closed the door.

It didn't matter if the lights were out. Darkness couldn't touch us. The drugs painted the air with colors, shapes, and shifting lights that no shadow could dim. I lay back on the carpet, dizzy and trembling, staring at the ceiling as patterns danced across it. Destiny stretched out beside me, her arm brushing mine, her breath steady.

"I feel whole," I whispered, the words tumbling out without thought. "Like everything's going to be okay."

"Maybe," she'd reply. Even in that kaleidoscope of light, her eyes still glimmered with shadows.

Months went by after that, and Destiny still wasn't convinced. One night she turned to me, her voice sharp, urgent. "I'm getting out. I can't stay here another night."

I hesitated, glancing at the closed bedroom door, listening for footsteps. "How?" I asked, my voice barely audible.

She pointed to the window. A two-story drop into the yard below. "We'll make it work."

We gathered every pillow and blanket we could find, dragging them across the room, tossing them out the window one by one. They landed in the grass with soft thuds, a pathetic pile that we convinced ourselves would be enough to break her fall. Destiny shoved a sock into her mouth, not to silence laughter but to muffle any scream if pain came. She looked at me, her face pale but determined, and said, "Push me."

My hands trembled against her back. "Are you sure?" I whispered.

She nodded once, steady, certain. "Do it. Don't think. Just count."

So I did. One. Two. Drop.

She fell fast, her body hitting the pile with a dull thud that made my stomach twist. I winced, leaning out the window, watching her curl into herself. She was definitely in pain—the way she clutched her side, the way her breath caught—but she didn't cry out. The sock muffled everything. She lay there for a moment, then rolled away into the shadows, disappearing into the night.

It turned out Destiny hadn't vanished into the night at all. While my friend Jessie was pulling up to get me, she had slipped into their van and hidden herself in the trunk, curled up in the dark like a secret waiting to be discovered. I didn't know it then, but she was already plotting her escape, already carving out a path that would take her far from the house, far from me.

Later, the truth came out in fragments. Jessie's mom noticed her purse was lighter, the cash gone, the credit cards missing. Panic rippled through the house, voices rising, accusations flying. At first, no one knew who to blame. But then someone remembered Destiny, remembered the way she had disappeared, remembered the silence that followed. I had been that someone, and the pieces fit together too neatly.

She had taken everything she could carry—money, cards, opportunity—and vanished. She went to Providence. That city became her refuge, her battlefield, her punishment. She was out there, surviving in ways that broke my heart to imagine. Trading pieces of herself for shelter, for food, for the promise of another day. Pimping herself out because she felt there was no other choice, because the world had given her nothing else.

I used to picture her walking down unfamiliar streets, neon lights flickering overhead, her face set in that same determined expression she wore the night she asked me to push her out the window. I imagined her clutching stolen bills, swiping cards that weren't hers, convincing herself it was all temporary. But Providence swallowed her whole. Weeks passed, then months, and the hope that she might come back shrank until it was nothing but a whisper we stopped saying out loud.

Jessie asked me once, late at night, "Do you think she'll ever come back?" The question hung heavy between us. I wanted to say yes, wanted to believe that love or family or sheer willpower would bring her back. But the truth was sharper. Destiny had chosen survival, and survival had taken her somewhere we couldn't follow.

And while Destiny was gone, I was still trapped in that house with eight of us crammed together: my dad and stepmom, my sister Ashlyn, my brother Bobby and his girlfriend Krystal, my niece Lexis, and my uncle Richie. Each person carried their own weight, their own shadows, but the one who made sure I never forgot my place was my stepmom Sheryl.

She hated me, and she showed it daily. She abused me openly, blamed me for everything, even when Bobby and Destiny stole from her. Somehow their mistakes became mine.

My life with her was a cycle of chores and punishments. Monthly wall washing. Daily sweeping and mopping. Chopping wood. Feeding chickens. Cooking dinner for the family. Doing the dishes until my hands were raw from hot water and soap. Taking out the trash—even though that was Bobby's chore, if he didn't do it, I was the one punished. Bobby was slim with blonde curly hair and blue eyes. He was the average older brother that didn't care much about his little sister or anyone. He liked women, sex, drugs. He was Sheryl's only son so in her eyes he did no wrong and somehow I did everything wrong.

Bobby was complicated. He never defended me when Sheryl lashed out, never stepped in when her rage turned me into a punching bag. He stayed silent, detached, as if my pain was background noise. But he wasn't cruel in the same way she was. He had his own world, his own chaos, and sometimes he let me slip into it.

Bobby loved parties. The house would fill with music, laughter, smoke curling through the air, bottles clinking against countertops. His friends sprawled across couches, their voices loud and careless, their energy electric. And even though he never stood up for me, he let me drink with them, let me hang out in the haze of their nights. It was his way of offering something—maybe not protection, but inclusion. He liked my friends too, liked the way they brought their own energy into the room, so it felt like a fair trade. He got company, I got escape.

But Bobby's interest in my friends wasn't innocent. He slept with them, sometimes openly, sometimes in whispers that reached me later. It was messy, uncomfortable, and yet in that house, nothing surprised me anymore. Boundaries blurred, respect was absent, and survival meant accepting things that should have been unacceptable. It was another reminder that in our family, love and loyalty were always tangled with deception.

And then there was Krystal. She was Bobby's girlfriend, sharp and sly, with a softness she saved just for me. She knew my parents wouldn't approve of her spending time with me, knew Sheryl would explode if she caught us together. So it became a waiting game—sneaking into their room when Bobby wasn't home, closing the door, and creating our own little world.

Krystal let me smoke weed with her, let me sink into the haze where everything felt lighter. She'd put on movies, the glow of the TV washing over us, the sound muffled by the walls. I remember the first time we watched *Grandma's Boy* together. We laughed until our stomachs hurt, quoting lines back and forth, the kind of laughter that felt rare in that house. For one night, it was the best movie night ever—just me and Krystal, hidden away, safe in the rebellion we carved out together.

She gave me something Sheryl never did: kindness. It wasn't perfect, it wasn't permanent, but it was real. In those stolen hours, I wasn't the scapegoat, the failure, the girl who couldn't do anything right. I was just a kid, watching movies, smoking weed, laughing with someone who saw me.

They didn't erase the abuse, didn't undo the venom of my stepmom. But they gave me moments to breathe, moments to remember that even in the darkest places, there were cracks where light could slip through.

I remember one evening vividly. I was making dinner, because that was my daily responsibility along with everything else. My glasses had broken months earlier, and my parents refused to replace them. They said I was faking, that I didn't need them, that I was making it up. So I squinted at the shelves, searching, fumbling. I couldn't find the canned corn. My stepmom saw me struggling, saw me fail, and her rage ignited. She smashed my head into the cabinets over and over until my vision blurred and my ears rang.

My sister Ashlyn was in the next room, but I knew she heard it. The bashing on the cabinets was loud enough to rattle the walls, loud enough to make silence impossible. Still, she didn't come. She didn't check on me. She didn't try to stop Sheryl. Ashlyn never did. She was too busy clinging to Sheryl, desperate for approval she would never truly earn. She wasn't Sheryl's biological daughter, and deep down she had to know she'd never be on her good side. But she chose Sheryl anyway, even if it meant leaving me alone in the fire because for her it meant she wasn't the one punished tonight.

"Stop acting stupid," Sheryl spat, her nails digging into my scalp as she smashed my head into the cabinets because I couldn't find the corn. Her cruelty was constant, not an outburst but a rhythm — the beat of my childhood. Endless chores piled on me, orders barked like a drill sergeant, and when Bobby made mistakes, she turned her fury on me instead.

My father never stopped her either. He would stand by, silent, complicit, as if cruelty was just another part of the household routine. He worked as an engineer, traveling to Venezuela for weeks at a time, and when he was home he spent most of his nights out with Sheryl. He wasn't the best — but I wanted to

17

believe he could be. I wanted to believe there was a version of him who would step in one day, who would protect me.

Instead, he let it happen. He would let all of it happen. His silence was worse than Sheryl's screaming. Her words cut, but his indifference hollowed me out. It told me I wasn't worth defending.

My dad would be home sitting in his chair,cigarette lit, eyes glazed, pretending not to hear to sounds coming from the room. Growing up without a dad I really just wanted him to love me.

That longing was the cruelest part. To ache for love from someone who would let me bleed. To admire a man who never stood up for me. To keep hoping, even when hope itself felt like another wound.

I had braces once. They were supposed to last two years, but after my parents refused to take me back to the orthodontist, the wires began slicing into my mouth. I recall Sheryl telling me to "deal with it." So one night, with my mouth raw and bleeding, I decided I would just deal with it my own way. I didn't have proper tools — only a pair of nail clippers. I pried the wire loose, clipped off the brackets, and filed down what glue I could. When it was done, the cutting stopped. They didn't even notice.

When they found out I was seeing a boy my age, they didn't ground me or yell. They didn't even sit me down for a lecture. Instead, they told me to go into my uncle Richie's room. *He* would "have a talk with me."

Richie lay in his bed, calm, almost gentle. "I'm not going to give you a hard time," he said softly. "You're giving me a hard time." Then he reached out and grabbed me. My body froze. My mind spun. He whispered "shhh," as if quieting me was part of the ritual. I was thirteen, confused, terrified, already broken down by Sheryl's daily abuse. And now my parents had delivered me straight into his hands.

After Sheryl discovered I was seeing that boy, she would later force me to take a pregnancy test. She shoved the test into my hand and ordered me to pee in front of her.

"I know what you've been doing," she sneered. "You're going to prove it right now."

My stomach twisted. "I can't," I whispered. "I can't pee with someone watching me. I get stage fright."

Her response was a fist to my face. The sting of her knuckles split my lip, swelling it instantly. Tears burned my eyes, but she stood there, arms crossed, daring me to resist.

So I did it — shaking, humiliated, forced to pee while she watched. I knew I wasn't pregnant, and of course the test came back negative. But the point wasn't the result. The point was control. She wanted to break me, to remind me that even my body wasn't mine.

Her fists left me with fat lips, swollen and tender, the kind of bruises that made teachers ask questions. She hated that. She feared exposure. So on those mornings, she'd let me stay home from school, not out of kindness but out of fear that someone might notice and she'd be caught. Pain bought me silence.

Richies abuse didn't stop that night in his room. Peterson's lake — a place that was supposed to be a secret spot for friends tucked behind acres of land in our backyard— became his hunting ground. He'd bring beer, hand it out to my friends, get us all drunk, and then corner me. What should have been a place of laughter and freedom turned into years of torment.

Meanwhile, the court battles left scars that never faded. My mom fought with everything she had to keep me, but when I stood in front of the judge, I told them I hated her. At the time, I thought I was proving something — thought I was choosing freedom. She had originally tried to keep me from having a relationship with him, and that resistance only pushed me harder toward him. I convinced myself that living with him was the answer, that siding against her was strength.

But when the truth revealed itself, when the mask slipped and his real colors showed, I couldn't admit what I had done. I couldn't face her with the reality that she had been right all along. I was embarrassed, ashamed, and trapped in my own silence. To confess would have meant proving her right, and I wasn't ready to hand her that victory — even if it meant carrying the weight of regret alone.

DCF stepped in during the battle and the cases were dropped. They warned both sides — my mom, and my dad with Sheryl — that if they kept fighting, both would be deemed unfit and I would be in foster care. The case was dropped, and I was left in limbo. No one won. No one protected me.

Sheryls control would run deeper than rage. She forced me to buy drugs at school — pills, weed, whatever she wanted. "If you want Jessie over," she'd say, "you'll get me what I need." Jessie was my lifeline, the only friend allowed in that house, and Sheryl knew it. She dangled Jessie's presence like a reward, twisting my desperation into obedience.

Sometimes she didn't stop with me. Sheryl even made Jessie bring weed. She knew Jessie's dad smoked, and she'd pressure her to steal from him. Jessie would do it, not because she wanted to, but because she knew how Sheryl was without her fentanyl patch and her weed to soothe her. Jessie understood the danger. She saw how volatile Sheryl became when she didn't have her fix, and she did what she could to keep some peace in my life.

That's when Jessie became more than a friend — she became my protector. I met her on the last day of eighth grade. We had

20

just dropped off our books, and instead of staying for the rest of the day, we ditched. It was instant — the kind of connection that doesn't need explanation. We walked six miles to the skatepark, laughing, singing stupid songs, chased by a bunch of ducks near a pond on the way home. We laughed so hard our stomachs hurt, and when we finally made it back — another two miles from the skatepark — I knew she was my best friend.

From then on, Jessie was the only friend my parents ever allowed over, even when I was "grounded," which I almost always was. She came almost every day when her parents allowed it, not just to hang out but to keep me safe. She knew what Richie was doing and hated him. She never told a soul, because she knew what would happen to me if the truth came out. Instead, she stayed close, helping me chop food in the kitchen, feeding the chickens and ducks, standing guard in her own quiet way.

One of the strangest, cruelest moments happened in that kitchen. One of the baby chickens had died, but Sheryl insisted it wasn't dead. She mocked me, telling me to feed it until it woke up. Jessie was there with me. We sat on the floor, holding the limp little body, trying to push liquid through a syringe into its open beak. The fluids just dribbled back out, pooling on the floor. It was terrible, heartbreaking, and absurd all at once.

But somehow, Jessie and I found humor in it. We laughed at the ridiculousness of seriously trying to feed a chicken we both knew was dead, because Sheryl was so unhinged she demanded it. It was the kind of laughter that comes from desperation, from knowing the situation is too cruel to cry about. Jessie's laughter saved me in that moment. She turned something grotesque into something survivable.

That was Jessie's gift — she could take the sharp edges of

my life and dull them with humor. Like the time we went to the movie theatre in Smithfield, the only one nearby. My dad had given me twenty dollars, told me to watch a movie and buy popcorn. We didn't care about the movie. We didn't even step inside at first. Instead, we met someone in the plaza to purchase weed, and we smoked ourselves stupid, running wild through the strip of stores, ducking into KFC, laughing so hard our stomachs hurt.

By the end of the night, we knew we had to play the part. We walked into the theatre just before the movie ended, slipping into the crowd so we could exit with everyone else. My dad was waiting outside, expecting us to come out like normal kids who had just watched a film. To sell the lie, we grabbed every "Bee Movie" poster we could find, convinced that carrying them would prove we'd been inside. But when he asked for the receipt, we froze. The posters didn't matter to him — the proof was in the paper. We lied, said we threw it out when we left, waving the stack of posters like they were evidence enough.

Later that night, still high and giddy, Jessie and I plastered my bedroom wall and ceiling with those posters. We didn't have tape, so we used lotion, smearing it on the corners to make them stick. One hundred "Bee Movie" posters staring down at us, ridiculous and perfect. Who uses lotion to hang posters? We did. And we laughed until our sides ached, until the absurdity of it all felt like freedom.

My birthday came up one year, but instead we were celebrating Bobby's. His birthday had been ten days earlier, yet my parents decided to throw his party on my actual birthday night. They swore later, the next month, that they had simply forgotten mine altogether. The sting of being overlooked sat heavy in my chest, but I refused to let it ruin me. Jessie was there, and together we decided to make our own celebration.

Jessie and me baked a cake in the kitchen, laughing as we threw it together, the chocolate frosting uneven, the candles replaced by matches, crooked. It wasn't perfect, but it was ours. It was proof that even if my parents forgot, I wouldn't let the day pass without marking it. Jessie made sure of that.

By the time night fell, we were drunk off jello shots, the kind of reckless fun that blurred the edges of pain. Destiny drove us there and her walk was exaggerated, wobbling like she was on stilts, and Jessie couldn't stop laughing at her , clearly shitfaced. We stumbled into a convenience store, carrying our chaos with us. Jessie wobbled too hard, crashing into a rack stacked high with snacks. The whole thing toppled, bags and boxes spilling everywhere. For a moment she was gone, blacked out, and then she popped back up, grinning like nothing had happened.

I don't remember if we bought anything. What I remember is the sound of our laughter echoing in that store, Jessie doubled over, Destiny still wobbling, and me standing there with the taste of jello shots and birthday cake lingering in my mouth.

It was hilarious, unforgettable, and in its own way, healing.

With Jessie, even rebellion felt like survival. She gave me moments where the pain didn't win, where laughter carried me further than despair ever could.

Not long after having livestock did the barn catch on fire. My brother had just gotten into an accident leaving the driveway, and my dad thought he could fix his car. He put the car in the barn, tinkering with it like he always did, but somehow a light fell and the entire barn went up in flames. I remember standing there, watching smoke curl into the sky, the heat pressing against my skin.

That was the day all my chickens died. Later, they found their bodies in a trash can inside the barn, as if they had tried to hide there. They were gone, reduced to ash and fragments, and the smell of burning feathers clung to everything.

Not long after, I stumbled into another kind of ruin. I dated this guy Travis once — if you could even call it dating. I met him through my distant brother Jason. Travis was twenty-four, already with a two-year-old son, and he lived reckless. He smoked weed with his kid in the car, bought me alcohol whenever I asked, and picked me up at all hours because he wanted something in return. He fed my addictions too, buying me boxes of Coricidin cold and cough medicine. The kids called it "triple C." I would take the whole box, chasing a high that blurred everything.

One night I snuck out, buzzing on that high, and Jason called Travis. Travis hesitated to meet him, and Jason accused him of being with me. Travis caught on to what was happening, but Jason convinced him to meet at some bar anyway. Travis had me hide in the back seat of his car, crouched low, while Jason set the trap. My parents showed up with Jason, told me to get out of the car, and I was so high I could barely walk.

Back home, Sheryl ripped me out of the car. We get inside and shes yelling at me. Everything is muffled because I'm still high. I must have been ignoring whatever she was saying because then she hurled a two-liter Coke bottle straight at my face. The impact knocked me flat, the weight of the bottle and the haze of the drugs combining until I nearly blacked out. Somehow I ended up in my bed, dazed, staring at the doorway. My dad stood there, his shadow stretching across the room. He didn't say a word. He looked at me like I was already ruined, like I wasn't worth saving.

It was around that time that my parents decided to introduce me to Spike. They had met him at some club they went to — they were swingers, always chasing thrills — and they decided he was a better match for me than the boy my own age. They preferred I date him, a twenty-six-year-old cokehead with chipped black nail polish, over someone my age who might have actually been safe. They brought him into my life like he was a gift, but really he was another weapon.

Spike wasn't perfect — he was bisexual, gothic, rebellious, and he had cheated on me before. His flaws were endless. But one night, he became something unexpected: a shield.

Richie crept toward my room, beer in hand, the smell of alcohol clinging to him like a warning. He was clearly coked out. He didn't realize Spike was there. He opened the door, his eyes narrowing when he saw us together.

"You shouldn't be in here," he said, his voice slurred but sharp. "I'm going to tell Sheryl and Dave you're having sex."

My heart pounded, but I forced myself to stay calm. "They know Spike's here," I said firmly. "They picked him. They said it was okay."

Spike sat beside me, silent but present, his dark eyes fixed on Richie. For once, his presence gave me strength.

Richie hesitated, his beer dangling loosely in his hand. He wasn't expecting resistance. He wasn't expecting me to speak back. I looked him straight in the eye and said, "If you don't leave my room right now, I'll tell Spike — and everyone else — the real reason you just came in here."

The words hung heavy in the air. Spike shifted, his jaw tightening, and I knew he understood enough. Richie's face changed, the bravado slipping, replaced by something uglier — fear, maybe, or shame. He backed out of the room, muttering under his breath, and disappeared down the hallway.

Later, we heard him pacing on the stairs, his voice low but audible, calling escorts. His words were disgusting, his presence unbearable. But at least that night, he didn't come back.

Jessie hated Spike too. She knew about his cheating, knew about the guy he had been with, and she never let me forget it. She gave him a nickname — "Floppy Fish n Balls" — and every time she said it, we laughed until our sides hurt. It was cruel, maybe, but it was ours. We picked on him together, mocking him, turning his betrayal into something we could laugh at instead of cry over. Jessie's humor was another kind of shield, a way of taking back power from the chaos.

Spike saved me that night, yes, but later he betrayed me in ways that cut just as deep. He cheated on me with the Burger King manager — a man he met while working as a McDonald's manager. It was almost absurd, the overlap of fast-food uniforms and secret affairs, but the pain was real.

And Richie... he was another kind of betrayal, one that left scars I carried in silence. I was in the basement with him and my brother one time, all of us smoking weed. My uncle insisted I give him a "shottie" — blowing smoke into his mouth. But when the time came, he twisted it. He said, "No, you're going to take one," and my brother held me upside down while Richie blew the smoke into my mouth.

When my brother set me back down, Richie told Bobby to make a call — I think about buying coke. I was so lightheaded I couldn't move. That's when he stuck his fingers down my pants and started kissing my neck. I could hear Bobby calling someone upstairs, his voice echoing in the kitchen, and once again I felt trapped. Looking back, I was numb. I don't know why I felt I couldn't scream anything to Bobby in that moment.

I didn't know what to do, so I just let him do it. Whenever he wanted.

Bobby would come back down the stairs and my face would be red, my neck raw from Richie's scruffy, gross old-man face. My pants would be wet. And I would sit there, silent, carrying the weight of it all.

Richie's cycle was never ending, even after he moved out, and the silence around it was suffocating. The only other person I could lean other than Jessie was my guidance counselor, Mr. Alcott. He was an old man with a long white beard, kind and gentle, looking almost like Santa. He listened when no one else did. He told me that as long as I didn't directly say I was on drugs or being abused, he wouldn't be forced to report it. So I spoke in hypotheticals, crying to him daily, pouring out pieces of my pain, in ways that didn't cross the line.

He gave me late class notes, excuses for skipped school, small mercies that helped me survive. He knew enough about my home life to understand that telling anyone wouldn't save me. And he also knew something else — that I was planning to run away. He knew I had tried before, and he knew I was planning again. But this time, he understood it wasn't just about escape. It was about bettering my future, about leaving them behind for good.

In his quiet way, he supported me. He didn't stop me, didn't shame me, didn't tell me it was impossible. He saw the truth: that survival for me meant leaving. And even if he couldn't rescue me, he gave me the dignity of being seen, of having someone acknowledge that my dreams of a different life weren't foolish. They were necessary.

At sixteen, I finally broke. My friend Karina from school—the girl with the pretty straight brown hair and the easy smile, the one who loved to party but was somehow still one of the kindest people I knew—was the one who helped me escape. She was popular, the kind of girl everyone seemed to know and want around, with a whole circle of friends orbiting her. But beneath all that shine, she was also genuinely a kind soul. She was a good friend, and she wanted to help. And somehow—against all odds—I was always one of the people she chose to show up for.

We were strategic. Karina had me meet her at a Cumberland Farms not far from where I was living. That night, I pretended I was just taking out the trash while making dinner. I left the stove on, praying Sheryl would come out to check on me soon. My bags were stuffed with clothes, makeup, notebooks — everything I could carry disguised as garbage. I sprinted past the church, past one other house, until I reached Cumberland Farms. Karina was waiting.

"Get in," she said, and I did.

I hid at Karina's house for a week, breathing for the first time in years. But hiding meant more than just staying quiet — it meant sleeping in her closet, curled up in the dark, waiting for the hours to pass. I could only slip out for bathroom breaks once school time was over, because I was a runaway and her parents didn't know I was there. The closet became my refuge, a secret space where I could finally rest without fear of being found.

That's when I met Jarrett, through Karina. He was only twenty-two, wicked tall, with a calm steadiness that felt different from anyone else I'd known. He took me from Karinas. His parents were sweet, and his mom — even while battling breast cancer — never stopped laughing, never stopped sharing her warmth. She made me feel welcome, like I had a place I could temporarily call home. For the first time, I felt like someone was protecting me instead of exploiting me.

Jarrett was a decent guy. He drove a black Accord, and throughout my time with him we would take ecstasy together. He'd bring me to private clubs that didn't ask for ID, and we'd dance until the sun came up, the music pounding through our bodies, the night stretching endlessly. He gave me shelter, yes, but he also gave me fun — a way to feel alive again.

Eventually, Jarrett gave me space until I was ready to call my sister. That call was the turning point. My voice shook as I told Alyssa what she needed to know, where to find me. She didn't hesitate. She came, picked me up, and brought me straight to my mom. My mom already suspected abuse, already carried the weight of knowing something was wrong, but hearing it from me — hearing the truth — mattered. So I eventually told her everything.

For a while, I was safe. I had moved in with my mom and was attending high school in Massachusetts, trying to build something that resembled a normal life. That's where I met Miguel. We crossed paths one day in detention — both of us stuck there for reasons that didn't matter once we started talking. He had this easy charm, the kind of words that made you feel seen, and I knew then that he would forever be a part of my life.

But safety never lasted long for me. My mom's boyfriend kicked me out after I accused his son of stealing my weed. His son denied it, made me out to be the bad one, but the truth was we were both smoking it. If he had just wanted to be honest, we could have smoked together instead of him taking my stuff. That fight ended whatever fragile stability I had at my mom's.

So I left with Miguel, and we stayed at this lady Renee's

house for a while. Her place became another temporary refuge, another stop in the cycle of running and hiding. It wasn't stability, not really, but it was somewhere to exist. Renee was an alcoholic, and the only reason we were allowed to stay there was because her daughter and I went to the same school. That connection gave me just enough cover to slip into her household without too many questions.

While I lived there, I paid rent in booze by working for scraps at Plainridge Racecourse, back before it turned into the casino it is today. My days were spent cleaning horse stables, the smell of hay and sweat clinging to me. Sometimes I'd drink with this woman Sandy, another worker, and if I got too drunk I'd collapse into the stalls and nap beside the horses. I bathed them, fed them after races, and prepped them for competition, strapping on their gear with hands that shook from exhaustion or alcohol.

I remember watching the way jealousy played out among riders — how people would drug test horses after races, suspicious of each other, desperate to prove someone was cheating. It fascinated me, the lengths people would go, the hidden rivalries beneath the surface. It was strange, but also strangely comforting, to know that even in that world of speed and competition, people were just as messy and flawed as the ones I lived with.

We left Renee's after one night outside her apartment changed everything. The police stopped me, Miguel, and this kid Bishop while we were sitting in a car in the parking lot.

We'd just handed off a small bag to the older woman who lived upstairs when the cruiser pulled in. They said they smelled weed, which they used as their reason to search the car. They found an ounce of marijuana, and that was enough to set the whole chain of events in motion. Bishop had just gotten a DUI, so he couldn't take the fall. Miguel, always quick to charm but quicker to disappear when things got serious, didn't want the trouble. He shrank back, silent, leaving me to carry the weight. So I said it was mine.

The cops didn't care about the truth, only about the ounce of weed they had found. And in that moment, I realized how easily I could be sacrificed — how quickly people I trusted could step aside and let me burn. Renee hated the police, hated the attention they brought, and when she heard what happened, she kicked us out without hesitation. No second chances.

So once again, I was uprooted. Miguel and I had nowhere steady to go, and that's when we ended up back at my dad's. But this time it wasn't the house — it was a camper parked on a friend's lawn, a makeshift shelter that felt more like a holding cell than a home. Miguel was living there too. He didn't have a steady job, but he sold weed, and Sheryl smoked it, calling it "payment" for letting him stay. For a while, that arrangement kept things quiet, or at least gave the illusion of peace. Beneath it all, though, the same chaos lingered, waiting to surface.

Miguel was different from the others. He listened. He believed me. He saw the cage I was trapped in, and he wanted to help me break out of it. At seventeen, I thought he was my knight in shining armor. We whispered plans late at night, sitting on the thin camper mattress, dreaming of a life beyond Sheryl's control.

But then everything collapsed. They accused Miguel of stealing ten thousand credit cards from the neighbors. It was a lie, but they clung to it. They kicked him out, and then they turned on me. They stripped away everything — my phone, my computer, Miguel's computer — until I had nothing left but silence.

I remember sitting in that camper, staring at the empty space where my things had been, feeling the walls close in. The air smelled of stale smoke and damp wood. Sheryl's voice carried through the thin walls, sharp and accusing, while my dad stayed silent as always. That was the last time I lived there.

I devised my plan to leave for good.

Burger King became my escape route. My dad dropped me off for work like usual, but Miguel had already contacted my mom. I remember standing behind the counter, the smell of grease and fryer oil clinging to my clothes, when I saw her car pull up. My mom and aunts husband James were there, waiting. My chest tightened. This was it.

I climbed into their car, leaving behind the camper, Sheryl's screams, and Lexis's tears.

Lexis was only four years old then, but my bond with her had started the moment she was born. Ashlyn was her mother, but she couldn't care for her the way a baby needed. From the very beginning, I stepped in. I was the one who held her, soothed her, tucked her in at night. I read her books, played dollhouse games, made the "bizzing" sound on her back to help her fall asleep. I pushed her on the swings until she squealed with joy. I tried to give her a world bigger than the camper walls.

When I escaped, Sheryl threw half my clothes outside, screaming that there was nothing else. None of the money I had given her, none of the valuables she had taken from me. Just rage, just blame. "How could you do this?" she spat, pointing at Lexis's crying, blaming me for her pain.

I hated myself for that moment — for Lexis's crying, for leaving her behind. I wanted to take her with me, but she wasn't mine. I knew I just needed to get safe.

Even now, decades later, I still think of her. I think of the little girl who clung to me, who trusted me, who deserved so much more than what she was given. I think of the promises I whispered to her, the books we read, the walks we took, the dollhouse games we played. She was my light in that dark house, the one person I could pour love into without fear.

Sometimes I wonder if she remembers those nights, the "bizzing" sound on her back, the way I tucked her in when Ashlyn couldn't be bothered. I wonder if she remembers the parks, the swings, the way I pushed her higher and higher until she squealed with joy. I wonder if she remembers the stories, the voices I gave to dolls, the way I tried to make her world bigger than the camper walls.

And my mom — the one I had once told a judge I hated — was the one who came back for me. After Karina helped me escape, after Jarrett sheltered me, after my sister brought me back to her already, she didn't hesitate. She and James were the ones who pulled up to Burger King that day, the ones who gave me my final way out.

That escape was the end of one life and the beginning of another. Sheryl's cruelty, Richie's hands, Jessie's laughter, Spike's double-cross, Karina's rescue, Jarrett's shelter, my sister's courage, Miguel's belief, , my mom's return — each of them stitched into me, scars and light alike.

This is the story of how I survived. And how, even in the darkest places, I found reasons to keep going.

3

Between Chaos and Consequence

Miguel and I were a team at one point. In my mind, he was my knight in shining armor — the one person who believed me when no one else did. I thought having him meant I'd never be alone again.

After leaving the camper at Dad's for good, Miguel and I ended up at my aunt's house. Technically, it was my grandfather's home, but as Poppop grew ill with cancer, she took control of it. She pushed him into the basement, claiming the rest of the house for herself. Her name was Claire. At the time, I was simply grateful she allowed us to stay. I had nowhere else to go, and even though I already knew how mean-spirited she could be, I convinced myself I could endure it if it meant having a roof over my head.

Claire's house itself was chaos wrapped in filth. She and her husband smoked constantly, the air thick with stale cigarettes. Dust coated every surface, as if the place hadn't been cleaned since my grandmother died. They were still living rent-free. My memories of that house as a child were always the same: the heavy smell of smoke, the haze that clung to the curtains, and the sound of slot machines ringing from an ancient computer with a massive screen. That machine was always running, always flashing, as if it were the heartbeat of the house. Meals were chaotic too. Plates piled in the sink, sticky counters, ashtrays overflowing. I'd sit at the table, trying to eat quickly, while Claire barked orders at her kids or lit another cigarette. The smoke curled into my hair, into my clothes, until I carried the smell everywhere I went.

Claire had four kids — two of her own and two from her husband's previous marriage. Their biological mother was lost to heroin, living somewhere on the streets. The kids had been born into addiction, but on the surface they seemed okay. What stood out about Claire was the way she carried herself. She thrived on tearing people down. She would openly cuss people out, mock them, or make cruel jokes unsolicited. And yet, in public, she wore a mask. To the PTA at school, she pretended to be mother of the year — polished, involved, the picture of parental devotion. She wanted everyone outside her walls to believe she was perfect, while inside she was cutting down anyone within reach.

It wasn't long before I began to hear and see how Claire treated Melinda, her eldest step-daughter. Melinda was only eight years old, small and fragile, her wide eyes filled with fear. I remember hearing the thud of her body against the wall one night, Claire's voice sharp and cruel. Then came the cries — Melinda's sobs, high-pitched and desperate — followed by the unmistakable sound of a hand smacking skin. My stomach twisted as I listened from the other room, frozen, knowing exactly what was happening but powerless to stop it.

That coldness reminded me of something I had experienced years earlier, when I was just a kid. My mom was dating a man named John, and he had two daughters around my age. We lived with them for a time, and I remember one day my mom dropped us off at my grandmother's house. My aunt Claire was supposed to be watching us. But her version of "watching" was cruel. She looked at John's daughters and told me they were trash, that they weren't coming inside. At first, I thought she was joking — I was only eight, too young to understand the weight of her words. But she wasn't joking. She meant it.

I watched as she forced them to stay outside until my mom came back to pick us up. Even though I didn't fully understand what I was seeing, I felt the sting of it. I couldn't admit to myself that my aunt was being cruel, not at that age. So instead, I stayed outside with them. I tried to make it seem like we were just playing, like it was all part of some game. I even convinced my cousin Nathan, my aunt's son who was my age, to come out too. We laughed and ran around, pretending it was fun, but underneath I knew I was covering up something ugly.

Nathan wasn't just my cousin — he was my first best friend. We were the same age, always together, always finding some-thing to get into. Bikes, skateboards, bugs in jars, backyard camping, video games that went on way too late. He came outside with me that day simply because I asked him to. He didn't know what my aunt had said or why John's daughters weren't in the house. We didn't talk about it — we were kids, and I was doing everything I could to pretend nothing was wrong.

That day taught me how some people use hostility as a form of power, how they twist authority into something ugly. Claire was the same way, just dressed up in adult disguise. She wanted the world to see her as a saint, but behind closed doors she was venomous. And my aunt, years earlier, had shown me the same truth: appearances can lie, and sometimes the people who claim to care the most are the ones who wound the deepest.

I tried to stay quiet about the abuse I knew was happening. I kept my head down, told myself it wasn't my place, told myself I couldn't afford to make enemies when I had nowhere else to go. I started working with another aunt in Newport, Rhode Island, cleaning houses as a maid. For the first time in years, things seemed to be looking up.

But chaos always found its way back. One afternoon, while I was at work, Miguel stayed behind at Claire's. At the time he wasn't working. He was asleep in our room when James — Claire's husband — stormed in. James demanded Miguel get up and do something for him, but Miguel didn't wake fast enough. James flipped out. Miguel called me, his voice tight with panic.

I rushed home immediately, but by the time I arrived the house was already vibrating with fury. I could hear the shouting before I even stepped through the door — sharp, jagged screams that didn't make sense, overlapping threats that blurred together. When I entered the room, it was chaos: hands flying, bodies tense, the air thick with rage. I couldn't tell what the words meant, only that they were meant to wound. The sound of feet stomping against the floor, the spit of curses, the heat of anger — it all collided at once.

Somehow, in the middle of that storm, something was said that pulled the words out of me, raw and unfiltered. My voice shook but cut through the noise:

"Stop!" I shouted, loud enough to pierce the chaos. "You're lucky we haven't called DCF on you already!"

The words hung in the air like a threat. James sneered, but it was Claire who snapped. Her face twisted with fury. She ripped the glasses off my face, threw them to the ground, and stomped on them until the lenses cracked.

"You dirty cunt," she spat, her voice dripping with venom. Then she kicked us out.

Just like that, we were homeless again. Miguel and I ended up sleeping in my Poppop's computer store. Poppop was kind enough to let us stay there as long as we needed. It wasn't much — just a back room filled with old monitors, towers, and wires — but I didn't care. I was just happy to have somewhere to stay, a roof over our heads, a place where we weren't being screamed at or shoved out the door. For almost a year, that cluttered little room became our home. We slept on the floor, surrounded by the hum of machines and the faint smell of dust and solder. There was one problem though: no shower. Miguel and I figured out quickly that we couldn't live without some way to clean up, so we found the nearest recreation center. It was a big brick building, the kind of place that offered everything — gyms, basketball courts, after-school programs — but for me, the showers were all that mattered. We'd take the bus there in the early mornings, when the place was quiet and the halls echoed with emptiness. The showers were tiled, the water hot, and for a little while I could wash away the grime of sleeping on a shop floor. It felt like luxury, like stepping into another world where I could pretend I was just a normal girl starting her day. Miguel always came with me. He wasn't just my partner in survival — he was my partner in everything. We were young, reckless, and deeply connected. Even in those stolen hours at the recreation center, we found ways to be close, to remind ourselves that we were more than just kids scraping by. The quiet of those mornings gave us privacy, and in that privacy we built our own little world. For me, those showers weren't just about hygiene. They were about freedom. About claiming something normal in a life that had been anything but. About laughing with Miguel as steam filled the room, about feeling like we had outsmarted the world by finding a place where no one bothered us.

Eventually, a studio apartment above the bar next door opened up. It belonged to one of Poppop's friends, and the rent was only $150 a week. Compared to everything we had endured, it felt like a palace. A place of our own. A chance to breathe.

The studio wasn't much. Just a single room with a lock on the door and a bathroom awkwardly connected outside, down a short hall. It felt more like a borrowed space than a real apartment. But to us, it was heaven — and it was ours.

Tommy lived next door in the other studio. He was older, quiet, and kind in ways that mattered. He bought us basics — shampoo, conditioner, soap — things we couldn't afford but desperately needed. He even let us rig his Wi-Fi so we wouldn't have to pay. Compared to my aunt's chaos, this studio and Tommy's generosity was a miracle.

The bar downstairs was loud, especially on weekends. Fridays and Saturdays, the music and shouting started at eight and didn't stop until after one in the morning. The bass rattled the floor, voices spilled through the walls, and sometimes it felt like the whole building was shaking. But I didn't mind. It was alive.

Living above the bar was fun for a while. Miguel and I liked to think we brought customers. I was young, pretty, and Miguel was sharp and funny. Together we had a way of drawing people in, making them laugh, making them stay. They'd come back not just for the drinks, but for us. Sometimes we'd even take them upstairs, into our little studio, where the party continued in our own way.

One night, we ate mushrooms and went down to the bar. The world bent and twisted, colors sharper, sounds heavier. I looked across the room and froze. Sitting at the bar was a skeleton, ordering a drink. My heart stopped. I bolted out of the bar and ran next door to Poppop's computer shop.

"Poppop!" I gasped, still wide-eyed. "There's a skeleton in the bar!"

He looked at me, calm as ever, and raised an eyebrow. "Are you on drugs too?"

That broke the tension. We both laughed, me half-hysterical, him shaking his head at me. "That's not the point!" I insisted between giggles. "She was scary — a skeleton!" He chuckled again, muttering something about Penny, his girlfriend. But to me, all I could see was a mean, old skeleton sitting at the bar, ordering a drink like it was the most normal thing in the world.

Living above the bar meant I could slip next door to Poppop's shop whenever I wanted. I'd sit with Poppop and his old buddies, and we'd get high together. They had these big vaporizers, filling the room with thick clouds of weed smoke. We'd laugh, talk shit, and tease his friend Jimmy. If it wasn't Jimmy, it was Ed, and we'd hit the "bullshit" button just to make fun of whatever nonsense they were saying.

Those nights were safe. They were stable. For once, I wasn't bracing for Sheryl's fists or Richie's hands. I wasn't hiding bruises or swallowing fear. I was just... living.

I was still working as a maid in Newport, scrubbing floors and polishing furniture, but it felt different now. I had a place to come home to. Miguel had finally gotten a job at Domino's, delivering pizzas with his sharp wit and easy charm. We were building something, however fragile. For the first time in a long time, things were looking up.

But the bar life came with shadows. Miguel started drinking more often. At first it was just part of the fun — the music, the laughter, the endless nights. But Miguel was epileptic, though not yet diagnosed, and the alcohol made his seizures worse. His mother didn't believe me when I told her. Miguel didn't believe me either. So he kept drinking.

Almost every night, after we laid down, he'd have grand mal seizures. He'd wake up vomiting, clutching his head, complaining of headaches. One night I was terrified he wouldn't wake up at all. He would seize, wake up confused and combative, then pass back out into another seizure. It went on like this for weeks.

I begged him to stop. I begged his mother to see what was happening. Neither of them believed me. And so he kept drinking, and I kept watching, scarred by the sight of the man I loved convulsing in front of me.

The drinking made him angry too. Suddenly everything was my fault — the bills, the stress, the money we didn't have. I was desperate to keep him calm, so I started web-camming for extra income. One night, a guy pulled me into a private session and held up a lighter, a match, and a can of Axe spray, asking me to tell him what to do. I threw out the wildest scenario and the only thing I could think of, and he actually did it. I walked away with two hundred dollars thinking, *thanks for the money, freak.* Anything to keep Miguel satisfied. But even that was never enough. He kept drinking, kept picking fights, kept finding new ways to blame me for his chaos.

I began to wonder if he was cheating on me. Almost every night we fought, but we always made up with sex — a lot of it. I wanted him to be the man of my dreams. I wanted to believe in our future together, if only he could stop drinking.

Then came the night he drank himself into status epilepticus. His body was shutting down. The doctors told me if I hadn't called 911 and had him rushed to Rhode Island Hospital, it could have been much worse. He almost needed a new kidney, almost went into dialysis forever. He almost died.

The sterile white walls, the beeping machines, the smell of antiseptic — all of it should have been terrifying. And it was. But it was also where we clung to each other harder than ever.

We were reckless, desperate, and young. In that hospital bed, with IV lines taped to his arms and monitors blinking beside us, we crossed a line. We had sex while he was still recovering, while the nurses walked the halls outside. It wasn't about lust. It was about defiance. About proving to ourselves that we were still alive, still connected, still ours. In that moment, we weren't patients and caretakers, we weren't broken kids fighting a disease. We were just us. And for a few minutes, the fear faded.

A couple of months later, everything changed.

The night before, I had been drinking. My cousin Nathan had slept over in the studio above the bar. I woke up sick, my stomach twisting, my head heavy. That morning, I had a nightmare — vivid and suffocating — that I was pregnant. I brushed it off at first, told myself it was just the alcohol, just my imagination. But the feeling wouldn't leave.

In that tiny studio, with its cracked walls and the muffled sound of the bar below, I took a test. My hands shook as I waited, the seconds stretching into eternity. And then the result appeared. Positive. The test in my hand was small, plastic, ordinary — yet it carried the power to change everything.

I stared at it, my heart pounding, my breath caught in my

throat. Pregnant.

I walked over to Miguel, still asleep, his body sprawled across the bed. I nudged him awake, my voice trembling but steady enough to carry the weight of what I held in my hand.

"Here," I said softly, placing the test beside him. "You may want this."

That single piece of plastic carried the power to change everything — our life above the bar, our reckless nights, our fragile survival.

For me, it was the beginning of something new. For us, it was the moment the world shifted. The air in that studio above the bar felt different. Heavy. Charged. The muffled bass from the bar below rattled the floorboards, but all I could hear was the pounding of my own heart.

He blinked, confused, his hair messy, his eyes still fogged with sleep. When he realized what it was, his face shifted — first shock, then something unreadable. I couldn't tell if it was fear or joy. Maybe both.

I didn't know what to do next. My body felt like it was floating, untethered. So I picked up the phone and called my father. I don't know why. Maybe I thought he'd surprise me, maybe I thought he'd finally be the parent I needed.

"I'm pregnant," I said, my voice trembling.

There was a pause, a silence that stretched too long. Then his words came, sharp and cold: "Take care of it."

It felt like a knife sliding straight into my chest. I hung up, numb, staring at the cracked walls of the studio.

The next person I told was my grandfather, Poppop, next door at the computer shop. He listened quietly, his weathered hands resting on the counter. He hinted at the same thing, though in his own kind way. "You don't have to do this if you're not ready," he said, his voice rough but gentle. Then he added, with a crooked smile, "No matter what, I'll love you. Even if a little terrorist comes out of you from Miguel."

It was his humor, his way of softening the blow. But underneath it was love. He didn't want me to suffer, but he wanted me to know I wasn't alone.

My mom didn't take it well either. Her face carried disappointment, worry, fear. But she never once mentioned abortion. Not once. That silence was its own kind of support.

Miguel's mother Mera, though, was furious. She had always hated me. She said I was bad for Miguel, that I ruined him. Back when we went to high school together for a short time, he'd get detention and bad grades. He stayed back three times. She never realized that I was a straight-A student, on the honor roll, that even when I skipped class I still managed to get the work done. She didn't care about that. She only cared that I wasn't the girl she wanted for her son.

She hated that I'd sneak into her house when Miguel and I first started dating. She hated that I was American and they were Brazilian. She made sure I knew, every chance she got, that I was not her son's first choice.

So when she found out I was pregnant, the only reasonable thing she could come up with to have control over the situation was to force us to move out of our apartment above the bar and into her house. She said above the bar was no place for a baby. And in that, she wasn't wrong.

I agreed. Even though I knew she and her husband hated me, I said yes. I said yes for the sake of giving our future child a better life than I had.

The night we packed up the studio, I sat on the floor surrounded by boxes, listening to the bar below. The music thumped, voices rose in drunken laughter, and for a moment I thought about what we were leaving behind. The chaos, the fun, the danger. The nights of mushrooms and skeletons, the fights and the reconciliations, the seizures that were nearly killing him. That studio had been our palace, our sanctuary, our battlefield. And now it was over.

Miguel carried the last box down the stairs, his face set, his jaw tight. I followed, clutching the pregnancy test in my pocket like a secret talisman.

4

Walls That Weren't Mine

Moving into his mother's house felt like surrender. On the surface, it was everything I should have wanted — cleaner walls, quieter nights, a roof that didn't leak, and rooms that didn't smell of stale beer or cigarette smoke. But beneath that polished veneer, the tension was suffocating.

His mother's eyes followed me everywhere, sharp and judgmental, like she was waiting for me to slip. She spoke to me with clipped words, her tone dripping with disdain, each syllable reminding me that I was not welcome. Miguel's stepfather wasn't much better. He was cold, distant, a man who carried himself with the authority of someone who owned everything around him — including, in his mind, the right to decide who belonged in his house. And I knew from the moment I stepped inside that he didn't think I did.

The house itself was massive, almost intimidating in its size. They had a two-story garage that could have been a home on its own, towering like a monument to their wealth. Attached to the main house was another two-car garage, polished and gleaming, the kind of space most families would dream of. From the outside, it looked like stability, like success, like the kind of place where children should grow up safe and secure.

I should have been happy. I should have felt grateful. But I understood what it really meant: living here meant dealing with his mother and his family, people who hated me, people who had already decided I was unworthy of their son. The size of the house didn't matter. The shine of the floors, the neatness of the furniture, the smell of cleaning products — none of it could erase the hostility that hung in the air.

Every room carried that tension. The silence wasn't peaceful; it was heavy, like a storm waiting to break. I walked through the halls feeling like an intruder, like every step I took was trespassing. His mother's disapproval was thicker than the walls themselves, pressing down on me until I could barely breathe.

One of my earliest memories there was at the dinner table. Antonio, Mera, Devin, Marcus, even Mera's mother — all seated together, the air heavy with formality. The smell of roasted meat and garlic filled the room, but it couldn't mask the bitterness in the air. The clink of silverware against porcelain was sharp, deliberate, each sound echoing in the silence between us.

Mera turned to me with a smile that didn't reach her eyes. "Do you want something to drink?" she asked, her voice sweet but edged with challenge.

Relieved for a moment at what felt like kindness, I said, "Yeah, can I have water?"

She set an empty glass in front of me, her face twisting like I'd offended her. "That's not how we ask in this house. We say please. Now you can get it yourself."

The humiliation burned through me. My cheeks flushed hot

as I reached for the glass, my stomach twisting. The scrape of my chair against the floor sounded louder than it should have, drawing every eye to me. Then she leaned toward her mother and murmured something in Portuguese, her voice low but sharp. I couldn't understand the words, but I didn't need to. The tone told me everything. She was mocking me, cutting me down in a language I couldn't defend myself against. The rest of the table sat in silence, forks paused mid-air, watching, pretending not to see what was happening. That was her way — constant little cuts, constant reminders that I wasn't good enough.

Antonio's hostility wasn't just in his presence — it showed up in the smallest things. One time, he sent Miguel and me an email so long it read like a book, a tirade about how much he hated Skitzo, my dog. We had both been working, and Skitzo had barked in his cage while we were gone. Antonio's words poured out like venom, line after line: *"This dog is a nuisance. Do you know how unbearable it is to hear him bark for hours? You're irresponsible. You don't belong here if you can't control him."* It went on for pages, as if the sound of a dog barking was proof of my failure. But Skitzo had to stay in the cage when we weren't home — it was the only way to keep him safe. Antonio didn't care. His email wasn't about the dog; it was about control, another reminder that even the smallest part of my life wasn't welcome in his house.

Devin, Miguel's older stepbrother, was thirty-two and still living under their massive roof. He came off as a nerd, but not the harmless kind — more of a creep, the kind you never saw with a girlfriend, always lurking in the background, his presence unsettling. He hovered in doorways, lingered too long in conversations, his eyes never quite meeting yours. Marcus, five years younger than me, was the typical teenager: partying, playing video games, wasting hours in front of a screen. He idolized Miguel, copying his habits, looking up to him as if he were the model of manhood. Together, they filled the house with noise, but none of it made me feel less alone.

I tried to adapt. I told myself if I could just learn their language, maybe I'd belong. So I picked up scraps of Portuguese, repeating words I overheard, practicing phrases under my breath. I wanted to understand what they said when they muttered about me, wanted to bridge the gap between us. But no matter how many words I learned, the tone never changed. Their language was sharp, their laughter edged with disdain.

When Mera and Antonio went on vacation, I tried to prove myself by maintaining their fancy house. I scrubbed floors, polished counters, dusted furniture until my hands ached. I wanted them to come home and see effort, see gratitude, see me as someone worthy of being there. But the silence when they returned told me everything. Nothing I did would ever be good enough.

Miguel and I started working together at Friendly's once. It was nearby, and after moving into his parents' house I was no longer cleaning houses. Friendly's paid minimum wage, but it was something. I worked as a fountain girl, scooping ice cream, building sundaes, hoping customers would sit at the counter where I worked so I could earn a tip. Every dollar mattered. I saved every penny I could, tucking money aside for our future child.

When I found out I was having a girl, the weight of respon-sibility hit me harder than ever. I knew I had to protect her. I knew she would look at me and wonder what love was. And if all she saw was the kind of love I had accepted — the kind that

49

hurt, the kind that broke me — she would fall into the same footsteps. I couldn't let that happen. I needed to protect her from repeating my mistakes.

Miguel was still having seizures and drinking, though not as bad as he had at the studio. Instead, he spent most of his time smoking weed or playing video games with his brother. I watched him waste hours in front of a screen, controller in hand, while I carried the weight of our child inside me.

I had a dog too — Skitzo. Walking him outside their house every morning started wearing me down during the pregnancy. Between the morning sickness and the discomfort of carrying a baby, even the simple act of walking half a mile so the dog could relieve himself felt like a battle. And every time I stepped outside, I risked confrontation with Miguel's stepfather. His presence was a shadow, a reminder that I didn't belong, that even the dog wasn't welcome.

And yet, every night, I pressed my hand to my stomach and whispered again: *"I'll protect you."*

Because even if the house rejected me, even if his family despised me, even if Miguel himself was lost in seizures and smoke, I had someone new to fight for. And that was enough to keep me breathing.

For a while, I worked at Friendly's, scooping ice cream and serving families who seemed so far removed from the chaos of my own life. I picked up holiday jobs too, anything that would bring in extra cash. Each paycheck felt like a small step forward, a chance to save for something more meaningful. I started to dream about college — not just as an escape, but as a way to thrive, to make more money, to build a future where I could be a good mom.

The holiday shifts were their own kind of madness. On Black

Friday, the stores were packed wall-to-wall, shoppers pushing carts piled high, their faces tense with urgency. I remember standing behind a counter, watching people fight over discounted shoes, their voices sharp, their hands grabbing at boxes as if survival depended on it. The frenzy was exhausting, but it also gave me perspective. Everyone was chasing something — bargains, status, gifts to prove their love — while I was chasing something simpler: stability.

And then came the last-minute Christmas shoppers. They would rush in with frantic energy, eyes darting, lists clutched in their hands, desperate to find the one thing they had forgotten. I'd ring up their items, smile through the chaos, and tuck away my own quiet hope that someday I'd be the one buying gifts for my child without fear of how I'd pay for them.

Those jobs were grueling, but they gave me more than money. They gave me a glimpse of the life I wanted — a life where I wasn't just surviving, but building. A life where I could stand on my own, provide for my child, and prove to myself that I was more than the whispers, more than the cuts, more than the girl they thought would never rise above.

I started saving money, little by little, putting it aside whenever I could. Miguel knew I didn't want to scoop ice cream forever. He knew I wanted more — I wanted to go back to school, to build a career, to prove that I could be more than the girl everyone whispered about. Nursing was the dream. I wanted to wear the scrubs, walk the hospital halls, and know that I was helping people while building a stable life for my child.

During my pregnancy, I managed to save almost eight hundred dollars to put towards school. It wasn't much, but to me it felt like a fortune — proof that I could plan, that I could fight for something bigger. Miguel, for all his flaws, somehow convinced his parents to help. They paid the remainder of my schooling for that year, and for the first time, I felt like the future wasn't just a fantasy.

I didn't get a degree, but I did earn my certification as a phlebotomist. I had gone in with nursing in mind, dipped my toes into medical assisting, and finally stopped at phlebotomy when life shifted again. Because in the middle of it all, I gave birth to my beautiful little girl, Ella.

After I had her, everything changed. I was able to find a job at Pinex Laboratories making fourteen dollars an hour — a huge increase compared to minimum wage and the fountain-girl tips I had scraped by on at Friendly's. That paycheck meant I could soon finally leave Friendly's behind and start my next chapter.

The job was mobile phlebotomy, and I didn't care that it wasn't glamorous. My car was junk — a beat-up white Hyundai Accent — but I drove it until I couldn't drive it anymore. I traveled everywhere: nursing homes, rehabilitation centers, individual houses. I drew blood in cramped bedrooms, in sterile hallways, in places where people were clinging to life or trying to rebuild it.

At first, I was terrified. In school, I used to get scared about hurting someone, about missing a vein, about causing pain. But after a month of running around, drawing hundreds of people a day, the fear melted away. I could do it in my sleep. My hands grew steady, my confidence stronger. Each patient was another reminder that I was capable, that I had carved out a place for myself in the world.

But while I was finding my footing at work, home life was another battle. We were still living with my in-laws, and every day felt like walking on eggshells. My mother-in-law, Mera, judged me constantly — even for breastfeeding. She wanted control over everything, telling me when I should feed Ella, when I should hold her, when I should let her cry it out. Nothing I did was ever right in her eyes. All I wanted was to keep Ella close to me, to protect her, but Mera disapproved of everything.

Miguel's other older stepbrother John didn't make things easier. He'd come by for Sunday brunch and call me fat, little digs that chipped away at me when I was already exhausted and vulnerable with a newborn. My patience was wearing thin, and the walls of that house felt smaller every day.

While I was still part time working at Friendly's, juggling shifts and motherhood. One time, Mera had to bring Ella to me at work because she wouldn't take a bottle. Ella cried for hours, and Mera grew furious, blaming me as if it were my fault. She stormed in, desperate, handing Ella over so I could feed her. The moment my daughter latched, the crying stopped, and Mera's anger only deepened. To her, it was proof that I had failed, when in reality it was proof of the bond I had with my child — a bond she couldn't control.

I stuck it out, hoping things would get better or at least buy me enough time to save so Miguel, Ella, and I could move into our own place. But the world never seemed to bend in my favor. Instead, everything shifted abruptly.

One night, close to 11 p.m., I got a call from my poppop. He was sick, battling stage 4 colon cancer, and the disease had left him in a haze. His voice was weak, confused, but urgent. He kept saying he wanted me to come see him before he went. I had already been there earlier that day, but something about the way he called made me believe he thought this was the end.

I woke Miguel's parents and asked if they could babysit Ella so Miguel and I could go. They were annoyed, but when I explained the circumstances, they reluctantly agreed. I asked Mera if she could put the baby monitor on since Ella was sleeping four floors above them, but Antonio overheard and exploded. He said absolutely not. I tried to compromise, asking if Mera could sleep downstairs with her instead, but that only made him angrier. I don't even remember what arrangement we finally agreed on — only that I left, determined to be with my grandfather.

When I arrived, Poppop was already on bed rest, already under hospice care. My aunt still had him tucked away in the basement, and that's where I sat with him for the next five hours. He was awake, though drifting in and out of a morphine haze, his words tumbling out in nonsense that somehow came out funny, almost childlike. He was so happy to see me. He hugged me with what strength he had left, his arms frail but full of love, and told me he was leaving soon.

But he didn't. He didn't die that night.

Instead, we shared something rare — a kind of joy in the shadow of loss. He rambled about all the bananas he was going to eat when he passed, and I laughed because I knew exactly what he meant. Bananas, to us, had always been code for marijuana. Back in my younger days at his computer store, he, me, and his buddies would vaporize weed and call it "eating bananas." I don't know why it stuck, but it did. And there in that basement, with the weight of death pressing in, we laughed about bananas.

He even chuckled remembering the time we got high upstairs by making tea out of it, shaking his head at how ridiculous we were. His laughter filled the room, raspy but genuine, and for a moment it felt like we were back in those carefree days, not sitting in a basement waiting for hospice to take its course.

Later, when he finally decided to go to bed, he looked toward the stairs and blinked in confusion. "They've turned into one of those round staircases," he said, pointing, "the kind that go round and round and never end." His voice was half-amused, half-bewildered, and I couldn't help but smile at the surreal image. The morphine had blurred the edges of reality, but even in that haze, he found wonder.

I held his hand, listened to his breathing, and waited. The weight of knowing what was coming hung heavy in the room, but I was grateful for those hours. Grateful for the nonsense, the laughter, the hugs, and the chance to remember him not just as a man fading away, but as the Poppop who once filled a computer store with smoke, tea, and laughter.

When we returned from that night with Poppop, reality hit hard. Antonio sent Miguel and me a text, furious that I had dared to ask him to put a baby monitor on. To me, it was a simple request — a mother's instinct, a way to make sure Ella was safe while I was away. But Antonio twisted it into something else. He made it sound like I had accused them of neglect, like I was saying they weren't properly watching her. In his mind, it wasn't about safety; it was about respect. And he decided I had disrespected him.

That single request was enough for him to decide we were out. He gave us thirty days, which might have seemed reasonable to anyone else, but I knew better. The message carried more than a deadline — it carried contempt, a reminder that in his house, even my concern for my child could be turned against me. I wasn't going to wait around for thirty days of tension, of glares, of silence that cut deeper than words.

I called my mom instantly, my hands shaking as I dialed. My voice cracked as I explained what had happened, and she didn't hesitate. "Come home," she said. Within hours I was gathering what I could of Ella's things and my own, stuffing bags with clothes, toys, diapers, whatever I could carry. Miguel stayed behind with his parents, caught between loyalty and convenience, while I searched for an apartment.

Within a week, I found one. A thousand dollars a month — more than I thought I could handle with all the other bills like electric and heat — but I had to take the chance. I had to believe Miguel would step up too, that he would make more money so we could provide for our family. It felt reckless, terrifying even, but it also felt necessary.

So Skitzo, Miguel, Ella, and I moved into an apartment in North Attleboro. It used to be a church, and you could feel it in the bones of the building. The ceilings were high, stretching upward like they were reaching for heaven. The hallways carried echoes, every footstep bouncing back at you, reminding you of the prayers and hymns that had once filled the space. The walls seemed to hold mysteries, whispers of sermons and confessions, secrets tucked into the cracks of old plaster.

It wasn't perfect. The rent was steep, the utilities loomed over me like another storm waiting to break, and the space itself was worn in places. But it was ours. For the first time, I felt like we were starting a new chapter.

That first night, I remember lying in bed listening to the creaks of the building, the way the wind rattled the old stained-glass windows that had been left behind. Ella's laughter echoed in the high ceilings, turning the place into something alive, something hopeful. Skitzo padded across the wooden floors, sniffing at corners like he was mapping out our new territory. Miguel sat with me, controller in hand, still half-lost in his games, but for a moment I let myself believe we were building something together.

The apartment carried a strange kind of peace. It wasn't the peace of silence or wealth, like Antonio's house had pretended to offer. It was the peace of ownership, of knowing that even if the walls were cracked and the echoes were loud, they belonged to us.

And for the first time in a long time, I felt like I could breathe.

5

Marys Saints

For a while, the apartment at Saint Mary's felt like freedom. The echoes in the hallways, the high ceilings, the stained-glass windows — they gave the place a strange kind of beauty, even if the walls were cracked and the rent was more than I could afford. But soon, the shine wore off, and the reality of living there began to show itself.

Our neighbor Patricia lived right next door. She was friendly enough, always eager to chat, but her apartment carried a smell that was impossible to ignore — the sharp, sour stench of cat odor that seeped into the hallway. It clung to her clothes, her hair, even the air around her. One afternoon she knocked on my door with a plate of meatballs, smiling proudly as if she were offering a gift. I thanked her, but when I looked past her into the dimness of her apartment — the clutter stacked high, the stains on the carpet, the smell that seemed to seep from the walls — I couldn't bring myself to eat them. I set the plate aside, guilt pressing against me, but fear stronger than hunger.

Meanwhile, Miguel had started disappearing. At first it was small — an extra hour here, a late return there. He'd say he was working, that the job demanded more of him. But soon the absences stretched into nights, whole stretches of time where he was gone and unreachable. I'd sit in the apartment with Ella, the echoes of the old church surrounding us, wondering where he was, wondering if "work" was just another excuse.

The building itself carried its own dangers. Down in the laundry room, tucked beneath the church's old foundation, I discovered a homeless man had made it his home. He had dragged trash into the corners, built himself a nest of discarded clothes and broken furniture. The smell of urine was thick, and when I stepped inside, I saw him crouched over a bucket, relieving himself like it was the most natural thing in the world. My stomach turned, fear rising in my throat. This wasn't just someone passing through — he had claimed the space, made it his own.

I couldn't ignore it. I called the cops, my voice shaking as I explained what I had found. They came, heavy boots echoing through the halls, and escorted him out. For days afterward, I avoided the laundry room, the memory of that bucket and the stench of urine burned into my mind.

Saint Mary's was supposed to be a sanctuary, a place where we could start over. But between Patricia's cat-soaked apartment, Miguel's unexplained disappearances, and the homeless man in the basement, the place felt less like a home and more like survival. Still, it was ours. And in the quiet moments, when Ella laughed and Skitzo curled at my feet, I tried to believe that even in Saint Mary's, we could carve out something resembling peace.

Life at Saint Mary's was never quiet, and the neighbors painted the building with their own colors. Veronica lived upstairs on the second floor. She had two cats that prowled the windowsills, but somehow her apartment never smelled like Patricia's. It was almost impressive — like she had discovered the secret formula for cat ownership without the eau-de-litter-box perfume. I used to joke that her cats were cleaner than most people. Veronica would laugh, shake her head, and say, "It's called cleaning, you should tell Patricia about it."

Her twelve-year-old son Leo was always darting in and out, his sneakers squeaking against the old church floors. Veronica worked late night shifts, and most mornings she was just coming home as I was heading out for work at 4 a.m. We'd meet in the hallway, bleary-eyed but grateful for the company. Sometimes we'd lean against the railing outside, smoke a couple of cigarettes, and laugh about the nosey neighbors who always seemed to know everyone's business. Veronica was cool — easy to talk to, no judgment, just a kind of tired camaraderie that made those early hours feel less lonely.

Down the hall lived Malik, a quiet guy with a calm presence. He and his girlfriend were potheads, but they minded their own business. You'd catch the faint smell drifting from their apartment sometimes, earthy and sweet, and I didn't mind it at all. In fact, it reminded me of freedom. I had quit smoking weed because of Ella — because being her mother meant being clear-headed, responsible, steady. But that didn't mean I was against it. The smell was comforting, almost nostalgic, like a reminder of a time when life felt lighter. It smelt good, and in a strange way, it reassured me that not every vice in the building was dangerous.

Then there was Brent. He lived on the second floor too, but his habits were impossible to ignore. Brent was a big-time coke user, and around 4 a.m., Veronica and I would sometimes catch glimpses of his bad habit. His door would crack open, the sound of sniffling echoing down the hallway, or he'd stumble outside with glassy eyes, jittery hands, and a restless energy that never seemed to settle.

One morning, as I was leaving for work, I walked out to find him leaning over my car. At first I thought he was checking something, maybe messing with the windshield. But then I saw it — a line of white powder spread across the hood, and Brent bent over, inhaling it like the world around him didn't exist. My stomach dropped, anger and disbelief mixing in my chest. My car wasn't just transportation; it was survival, the one thing I relied on to get to work, to keep food on the table, to keep Ella safe. And there he was, using it like a drug table.

One night, everything suddenly made sense. Miguel hadn't come home, and I tried to convince myself it was just another late shift, another excuse about work. But in the middle of the night, I woke to the sound of something wet hitting the floor. The hallway reeked, and when I stepped out, I saw vomit splattered across the walls and carpet. My first thought was Brent — it had to be him. He was always strung out, always stumbling around at odd hours.

I followed the trail, disgust rising in my throat, each step leading me closer to his apartment. But when I reached the door, it wasn't Brent. It was Miguel.

He was slumped there, pale and shaking, the mess leading straight back to him. That's when it hit me — Miguel wasn't just disappearing for "work." He had been with Brent. He had been drinking, doing coke, wasting nights that left me alone with Ella.

The realization cut deep. It wasn't just disappointment — it was a wound that split me open. I had been dumb, sand-blind, clinging to the idea of a perfect little family while raising our daughter. I wanted so badly to believe in us, to believe in him, that I hadn't been paying enough attention. I had ignored the signs, brushed off the absences, convinced myself it was stress or seizures or anything but what it really was.

And then there was the vomit. The smell was thick, sour, clinging to the hallway walls like a warning I couldn't escape. It turned my stomach, but it wasn't just the stench that made me sick — it was what it represented. Every splatter on the floor was proof of disloyalty, proof that Miguel had been lying, proof that the man I thought I was building a life with was unraveling right in front of me.

Standing there, staring at the trail that led to Brent's apartment, I felt the revelation press down on me like a weight I couldn't shake. It wasn't just Miguel's body rejecting the drugs — it was my heart rejecting the truth I had tried so hard not to see. I had wanted the fairytale, the perfect little family, the laughter in the high-ceilinged apartment, the hope that echoed in Ella's giggles. But instead, I was left with vomit to clean in the hallway, lies in the silence, and a man who was slipping further away.

After months of denial, Miguel finally admitted the truth. The nights he spent away weren't about work or stress — they were about drinking and coke, hours wasted with Brent. Hearing him confess was devastating, but it was also the first step. Lies had been stripped away, and now I had to decide what came next.

I knew the only way to help him, the only way to protect Ella, was to leave Saint Mary's. That building had been our temporary refuge, but the streets around it were filled with users, shadows of addiction on every corner. Ella shouldn't have to grow up in that. She deserved more.

Miguel promised he would get clean, and with that promise

we began looking for houses. I threw myself into the process, determined to carve out something better. I attended an FHA loan class, learning every detail I could about how to make it work. I worked with a realtor. While I hadn't saved much from my paycheck for a down payment, every year when I filed taxes and claimed Ella, I received a return of over four thousand dollars. That became my chance. I put it toward a down payment for a house I knew I had to buy.

The timing was right. The market was good, the area looked safe, and the school system was strong. I knew everything I was paying in rent would probably double once the mortgage, utilities, oil, and electric bills came in. But I didn't care. I couldn't risk moving into another rental where the same problems might follow us. Buying a home meant stability, meant giving Ella the life she deserved.

I told myself I'd make it work. I'd get another job if I had to. So while Miguel worked as a valet, I picked up a new position at QuantumCore Laboratories just two weeks before closing on the house. The new position offered me a couple more dollars an hour. The realtor warned me it might cause pushback if the lenders asked for current income, but because of my work history and consistency, there shouldn't be anything to worry about.

I remember the day of the closing vividly. Sitting across the table from the old homeowners, Louie and Lois, I could feel the weight of their goodbye. Louie had a green thumb — you could tell by the way he spoke about the garden, the pride in his voice. I had seen it during the open house: rows of flowers and vegetables, carefully tended, each plant a testament to years of care. Lois was sweet, her hands folded nervously, her eyes darting as if she wasn't ready to let go. Louie explained he was moving to Florida while Lois stayed in the area with their daughter. Were they divorcing? Was I buying this house because of someone else's failed marriage? Maybe. But it didn't matter.

What mattered was the moment I signed my name, the moment the keys were pressed into my palm. That was the first time I felt what true safety meant. Not borrowed walls, not temporary shelter, but home.

Moving into that home wasn't just about Ella's future — it was about ours. For me and Miguel, it felt like a chance to rekindle what we once had, to rebuild the love and trust that had been buried under lies, absences, and addiction. The day we carried everything inside, box by box, bag by bag, I felt more than the strain of lifting furniture or unpacking dishes. I felt the weight of every place I had lived before — every cracked wall, every hallway soaked in betrayal, every night spent wondering if survival was all life would ever be.

This house was never going to be like the others. It wasn't going to be another House of Lies, the kind of place where promises were made only to be broken, where love was twisted into control, and where survival meant silence. It wasn't going to be like the homes where I could be tossed out at a moment's notice — the way my mother's boyfriend had kicked us out, or the time Renee forced us to leave with nothing but bags and heartbreak. It wasn't going to echo the betrayals of the past, the manipulation and mistreatment I endured under roofs that were supposed to protect me but instead taught me how to carry fear like a second skin.

It wasn't going to be like the house where I learned that family could lie to your face and still call it love. Where I was made to feel small, voiceless, and disposable. Where the people who

64

should have protected me instead built walls of deceit and left me to navigate the wreckage. And it wasn't going to be like the place where Richard's shadow lingered — the chaos, the pain, the way his choices carved scars into my life that I carried long after leaving.

This was different. This was the final break, the last tie to all of that.

As I set Ella's toys in her new room, stacked groceries into unfamiliar cabinets, and watched Miguel wrestle the couch through the doorway, I told myself this was the line in the sand. The past would not follow us here. Every box unpacked was a step away from chaos, every nail hammered into the wall a promise that this house would hold love instead of lies.

I knew rebuilding wouldn't be easy. Trust doesn't return overnight, and love doesn't erase the damage. But standing in the middle of that living room, surrounded by half-opened boxes and the sharp scent of fresh paint, I felt something I hadn't felt in years: safety. This wasn't just walls and a roof. It was a declaration. A place where Ella could grow without shadows, where I could breathe without fear, and where Miguel and I could fight — not against each other, but for us.

This home would no longer carry the echoes of old pain. It marked the start of something new.

6

Cupcakes and Hidden Truth

The house quickly became the stage for my routines, the rhythm of survival and motherhood etched into every corner. Each morning I woke before the sun, coaxing Ella out of bed, brushing through her curls that framed her face like a crown. Her hair had a life of its own, bouncing with every step, and I loved the way it seemed to mirror her spirit — wild, free, untamed. She'd grin at me in the mirror, her smile so radiant it could light up the room, a reminder that even in the hardest moments, joy was still ours.

Packing her bag for daycare became a ritual, her laughter spilling into the hallway as she insisted on choosing her own outfit. Shed smile and twirl to show me her choice. That smile — wide, genuine, full of innocence — was the kind of beauty that made the weight of everything else feel lighter.

After work, I'd rush home to cook dinner, fold laundry, and keep the house in order. Ella would trail behind me, carrying her toys and dragging her baby blanket into the kitchen, her smile flashing as she asked if she could help stir the pot or set the table. Grocery shopping became a weekly ritual, lists scribbled on scraps of paper, bags carried in with Skitzo tugging at the leash, while Ella skipped beside me, singing silly songs. Her smile would turn even the most ordinary errands into something extraordinary.

Miguel worked too, but his hours were never set. Some nights he'd be gone until late, other days he'd be home in the middle of the afternoon, and I never knew what to expect. His schedule was a question mark that hung over us, leaving me to carry the weight of predictability alone. I was the one Ella could count on — the one who made sure she was fed, clothed, and safe.

Still, I held onto hope. The home was more than walls and a roof; it was a promise. A promise that the chaos of the past would not follow us here. A promise that Ella, her innocence, her beautiful smile, would grow without shadows. A promise that I could breathe without fear, and that Miguel and I could try to find our way back to each other.

The next few years slipped by faster than I could hold onto them. Ella grew in what felt like a blink — her curls longer, her smile brighter, her laughter filling every corner of the house. But while she was growing, the rest of my world was shifting in ways I didn't expect.

My Poppop had always been the one who held our family together — the steady center, the quiet strength, the person everyone trusted even when they didn't trust each other. Losing him to cancer left a hole nothing and no one could fill. After he passed, the foundation of our family quietly cracked, even if we didn't see it right away.

He had one sister, Aunty Marie. While she wasn't the glue or deeply involved in our lives — she was the aunt who always sent money, gifts, and cards on birthdays and holidays. Thoughtful, generous, but distant. Her love came in envelopes and packages, not in presence. And sometimes that kind of distance makes people project their own hopes, expectations, and motives onto you.

When she died, it wasn't her absence that shattered us — it was everything that happened after. The will. The signatures. The choices made behind closed doors. The way greed can turn blood into strangers. The way Aunt Claire stepped in to "help" and took control of everything before anyone could blink.

One minute she was in rehab, the next she was fading, and then she was gone. No time to question anything. No time to understand. Just decisions made quietly, and the rest of us left trying to make sense of it.

So while Ella was growing, I was carrying all of this — the grief, the betrayal, the questions. And through it all, I kept trying to build something stable for her. Something soft. Something safe. Something that didn't mirror the chaos I came from.

And just when I thought I had found a rhythm again— life reminded me that pain can also come from the person sleeping beside you.

Before I knew it, Ella was five, and I was standing on the edge of another chapter. But before the joy of a second child, there was another wound waiting for me. I found out Miguel was having an affair. The truth didn't come gently; it hit like a blade.

I discovered it only a couple of hours before our daughter's birthday party. My phone had died while we were in the store, and I needed to call my mom to pick up Ella. I had just finished a five-hour Saturday shift — one I picked up for extra money — and I was already drained. Miguel handed me his phone so I could make the call, and as I went to dial, the screen lit up with a notification: *"Shannon typing..."* on Snapchat.

I froze. The name was unfamiliar, but the timing was damning. I asked him who she was, and before I could even finish the question, he ripped the phone out of my hand. His voice rose, sharp and cutting, calling me crazy, screaming at me in the middle of the store where we were grabbing last-minute supplies for Ella's birthday. The fluorescent lights buzzed overhead, the aisles crowded with strangers, and there I was — humiliated, accused, stabbed by a truth I hadn't even had time to process.

Later, at the party, I made a choice. I wasn't going to ruin Ella's day. I wasn't going to let her fifth birthday be remembered for her parents' chaos. So I swallowed a few Xanax, washed them down with a shot of Jamenson alongside Miguel's brother, and slipped into a version of myself that could smile, laugh, and pretend. Honestly, I think I blacked out. The edges of the night fade when I try to recall them, but I know the party went well — I have the pictures to prove it.

I don't know who I became in those hours. A performer, maybe. A mother desperate to shield her child from the storm. I played my part well enough that no one suspected the stab I felt in my heart, the hollow ache that pulsed beneath every laugh, every smile, every candle lit on Ella's cake.

Only later did I learn who she was. Shannon. She was only eighteen, much younger than us at twenty-five. She had long, flat, straight hair that fell like a curtain down her back, the kind of hair that never seemed to frizz or fight against her. She was skinny, untouched by childbirth, her body still perfect in the way youth allows. She wore oversized glasses that barely fit her face, as if the world needed another reason to notice her.

I noticed her too — not because I wanted to, but because she made me feel inadequate. Standing next to her in my mind, I felt ugly, worn down, like I wasn't good enough. I had carried a child, carried a home, carried the weight of survival, and yet here was this girl, untouched, untested, and somehow enough to pull Miguel away.

When the affair came fully into the light, he left us for a couple of weeks, living with her and two other boys, like he had traded our family for some reckless experiment. And then, as quickly as he had gone, he realized he had messed up. He came back, begging, pleading for another chance. He told me he didn't want to end their friendship, but he would end the affair. The words shattered me. Friendship? As if betrayal could be softened by a different name. I told him no — not here, not in the home I had fought so hard to build.

He swore he had deleted her from everything, cut ties, erased the connection. And for a while, I let myself believe it.

A few months later, life shifted again. I found out I was pregnant with my second child — a boy. Alfonzo. His name felt like hope, like a new beginning, even as the cracks in our foundation still showed.

Four months into the pregnancy, I had an epiphany. If she had been bold enough to take what wasn't hers, then she would also be the one to hand me back proof that he was still mine. I wanted her to understand the truth — that while she thought she had him, he was still coming home to me. He had been with both of us, and I needed her to see that she was never more than a distraction.

For a moment, I made her feel like she mattered. I handed her the instructions, told her what to deliver to the baker, and gave her a role in something that wasn't hers to begin with. For that single minute, she could pretend she was important, that she had a place in the story. But I knew the truth — and I knew it would kill her to see what was inside that cupcake.

It was a boy. A baby boy. A new beginning that she would never be part of, no matter how close she had tried to wedge herself into our lives. The baker followed my directions exactly: the gender color hidden in the center, covered with white frosting so nothing would be revealed until the moment it was cut open. And she was the one who carried it, the one who arranged it, the one who had to stand there and watch as the truth unfolded.

I wanted her to see it, to feel it. To know that while she thought she had him, he was still mine. That she had lost. That her place in this story was nothing more than a footnote.

And in that moment, as she placed the cupcake in his hands and lifted the camera to frame the scene, it was as if the curtain had risen on a play I had written myself. The spotlight was on her, but the script was mine. For one fleeting instant, she could pretend she mattered — the messenger, the orchestrator, the one holding the secret. But she was only an actress in a role I had cast, a supporting character in a story that would never belong to her.

The cupcake was the prop, plain white frosting concealing the truth inside. The baker had followed my directions perfectly: the hidden color waiting in the center, a revelation timed for the climax. And when the knife cut through, when the secret spilled out, the audience — his friends, his coworkers — erupted in celebration. A baby boy. A new beginning. A life she would never touch.

She was forced to deliver it, to announce it, to watch as the joy unfolded without her. That was the cruelty of the performance — she had to play her part, knowing the ending was written

71

against her.

If betrayal had to be carried, then I would carry it like theater. Pain became performance, humiliation became spectacle. Let her watch, let her record, let her choke on the truth. Because fuck her.

Time passed, and the spectacle of the cupcake gave way to something far more profound — the arrival of another beautiful human. Delivered by C-section to avoid the complications I had endured with Ella, he came into the world healthy and strong. Breastfeeding became our quiet ritual, the hours where the world fell away and it was just the two of us. His tiny fingers curled against my skin, his breath warm and steady, and in those moments I felt a bond unlike anything I had known before. With Ella, I had learned how to be a mother. With Alfonzo, I learned how to be whole again.

Raising two children reshaped everything. Ella twirled through dance classes, her curls bouncing as she spun across the studio floor, her smile lighting up every recital. Alfonzo grew quickly, his laughter filling the house, his energy spilling into soccer games alongside his sister. Weekends became a blur of muddy cleats, sideline cheers, and dance costumes glittering under stage lights. By then, the house was full — two children, three dogs, and the endless noise of family life.

But beneath the joy, I felt the weight of responsibility pressing harder. I needed financial freedom. Miguel was still valeting, his income unstable, and QuantumCore Laboratories only paid me so much. I wanted more — not just for myself, but for the kids. I wanted security, a future where I didn't have to wonder if the bills would be paid or if the roof over our heads would hold.

I tried to move up at QuantumCore Laboratories, desperate

to carve out something better for myself and the kids. My boss approved the transfer, even signed the papers, and for a moment I thought I had finally broken through. After seven years of stability, I believed I was about to step into growth, into something more than just surviving.

But on my very first day in the new department, the director of pathology stopped me cold. He was tall and lanky, probably around sixty, with more hair than you'd expect for his age. His presence wasn't commanding, but his words carried a harshness that cut deeper than any shout could. He looked at me with disdain, his voice sharp and dismissive, and told me I didn't belong there. He said he hadn't approved the transfer, that I should go back to school — that's why QuantumCore Laboratories offered financial assistance, he sneered. Until then, I wasn't welcome to grow into the position my boss and future boss had already promised me.

It was humiliating. I felt small, worthless, like all the years I had given to that company meant nothing. Seven years of loyalty, of showing up, of stability — and in that moment, it all collapsed. I walked away from that encounter not just wounded, but changed. I no longer wanted stability if it meant being trapped. I wanted freedom. I wanted growth. I wanted out.

That experience lit a fire in me. I refused to stop. I started applying everywhere — every lab, every position, even the ones that demanded bachelor's degrees I didn't have. I figured someone, somewhere, would see me for more than a piece of paper. Someone would give me a chance.

And then one day, while I was at work, the call came. Novara Biotech Labs wanted to interview me. I read the role description and didn't understand half of it — GMP, sample testing, stability monitoring — none of it made sense. But I told myself if they were willing to interview me, they must also be willing to teach me. My resume made it clear I didn't know those systems, but maybe that was the point. Maybe this was the chance I had been waiting for. Within a month of that first interview I was about to quit QuantumCore Laboratories and start my next chapter with a 15% raise.

7

Toxic Authority

When I first started at Novara Biopharma, I thought I had finally broken free from living paycheck to paycheck. I thought this was the chance to grow, to step into something bigger. And in many ways, it was. Almost every employee I came across was kind, helpful, and willing to teach me. They answered my questions, showed me the ropes, and made me feel like I belonged. Honestly, if Laurie hadn't been there, I truly believe I could have thrived.

But Laurie was there.

Laurie was my boss. She was heavy-set, with eyes that seemed designed to dominate the culture of the place. She mocked employees behind their backs, gave me wrong directions, and made sure everyone knew I was "hers." The other employees avoided me because of it. By my third week, I was ready to quit. I even called my old boss at QuantumCore Laboratories — the door was open if I wanted to return. But I kept asking myself: *Am I really going to let this woman ruin my growth?* I had just started learning, just begun to feel powerful gaining knowledge. I didn't want to give up the money, and I didn't want to give up the chance. So I stayed.

The months that followed were a fog of brutality and manipulation. Laurie lied, falsified records, and pinned her mistakes on others.

I remember one time she had me searching for nine-month stability results to send copies along with the COA. She had me running all over the building, digging through files and desks, but wouldn't let me check her office. I spent most of the day retracing the same places, frustrated and exhausted. Divya, a girl in Quality Assurance, noticed me searching and asked if I had tried Laurie's office. She smirked and called it *"the lion's den."* I told her Laurie wouldn't let me check, she said *"Dont bother. It's not there."*

We waited until Laurie took a bathroom break. Divya kept lookout from her desk in the hallway while I slipped into Laurie's office. Within five minutes, I found the stability results sitting right on her desk. I hurried to scan them into the O-drive for future reference, then placed them back exactly where I found them with a note on top: *"9m stability results for Product Zen."*

When Laurie returned, she messaged me for a follow-up. I explained the results had been found — on her desk — and that they were scanned into the system so they couldn't be hidden or lost. Minutes later, she stormed to my desk, demanding why I had gone into her office. I told her plainly: *"They were found, and that's what matters."*

She turned to Trina, another colleague who worked under Tim's supervision, and asked if she had told me to do that. Trina said no. Laurie huffed, then after several loud complaints about me, she turned back to Trina and asked where the shipping forms for a customer were. Trina ignored her for a moment, then finally said, *"Sorry, I'm not used to being micromanaged. I'll have it complete by the requested date."*

Trina was short like me, but a bit heavier and with blonde hair and blue eyes. She was about my mom's age, but she carried herself with strength and independence. She was resourceful, helpful, and didn't like Laurie either. That day marked the beginning of our friendship — built on a mutual hatred for Laurie and a shared determination to survive her chaos. She was probably like 42 and clearly loved gambling at casinos and scratch tickets. I'd watch her come back from break with a handful of scratch-offs, sit down at her desk, and scratch them right there, the silver dust sprinkling across her papers. It was almost a ritual, a small rebellion against the suffocating atmosphere Laurie created. Watching her do it made me smile — proof that even in a toxic workplace, people found little ways to keep themselves sane.

Not long after, Laurie escalated her callousness. She had me gather documents from desks all over the building, pile them into one room, then snapped a picture and accused Tim, the director of quality, of negligence. Tim was fired for that. Watching him walk out the door was devastating — not just because he didn't deserve it, but because it showed me how far Laurie would go to destroy someone she didn't like. It was important to me to remember that moment, because Tim's story wasn't over. He would come back into mine later.

She backdated sample volumes, trained new hires in secret her way, and nearly caused a disaster when she handed Jen, the new girl, a draft protocol to label 2,000 samples. Laurie left for the day after giving Jen the protocol to follow. I caught the mistake before it reached QC, reported it, and while I thought I was doing the right thing, I was sent home the next day — as if

I was the one who almost created 2,000 labels with the wrong drug substance information.

And then came the personal blow. My daughter got sick — COVID. I did everything right: I called out, sent over a doctor's note, and stayed home to care for her. When I tested positive myself, I followed protocol and quarantined for ten more days. Instead of compassion, Laurie had me written up. In her eyes, even illness was a weakness to exploit. I remember sitting at home, exhausted from fever and worry, staring at the email that said *"written up"* and wondering how a company could punish someone for protecting their child.

It's funny to me because when I was hired by Laurie, I explained I was a mother. She told me in the interview that she was a single mother raising her daughter. She pretended to show compassion, but it was all a mask.

The breaking point came with shipping. Laurie gave me instructions to send 25 samples to a client. I followed her directions exactly — there was no procedure to tell me otherwise. Later, it turned out they weren't the samples that were supposed to go. She had me written up again, trying to pin the mistake on me. But this time, I fought back. I cc'd every higher-up name I had in the company, attaching the email chain that proved she had given me the wrong information. I showed them I had followed her orders, step by step, and that she was lying. Hitting "send" on that email felt like reclaiming my voice, even if I knew it might cost me everything.

For eight months, I documented everything — every discrepancy, every manipulation, every time she tried to erase the truth. My notebook and Teams screenshots became my shield, each entry a reminder that I wasn't crazy, that what I saw was real.

Eventually, the investigation came. Whatever the outcome

was, they told me I could be moved into a different position. It felt less like a solution and more like a way to sweep everything under the rug. Laurie's behavior was being looked at, but instead of accountability, they offered me relocation. I was reluctant — I had fought hard to prove myself in Quality Control, learning the ins and outs of raw materials, stability control, and buffer preparation. That was the work I loved. But the offer was for QC Micro, and I had to decide whether to take it or walk away entirely.

I told myself maybe this was a chance to reset. So I accepted.

My first day in Micro was nothing like I imagined. I walked in, trying to carry the weight of determination, but before I could even settle in, security stopped me at the door. HR — or rather, talent acquisition pretending to be HR — was waiting. She was skinny, with super short boy-cut hair, her tone sharp and cold. She told me I had two minutes to gather my things. No explanation, no compassion, just a dismissal.

I stood there stunned. After months of documenting Laurie's negligence, after reporting her lies and protecting the company from mistakes, this was how it ended. I knew what they were doing was illegal, but I was still naïve. I gathered my belongings, stepped outside into the sun, and cried.

The building behind me felt heavy, like it was swallowing the truth whole. And yet, as the tears dried on my face, I knew something else too: they hadn't erased me. Laurie had tried to silence me, but I had spoken. I had documented. I had fought.

But that was also the day I learned something I couldn't ignore. Management will always come first. It didn't matter how much evidence I had, how many lies I exposed, or how many mistakes I prevented. What mattered was protecting the hierarchy, protecting control.

I realized then it wasn't about what you know — it was about who you know. Connections carried more weight than honesty, and truth was disposable if it threatened the wrong person. Honesty didn't matter in this field. What mattered was total control, no matter how they got it.

That lesson cut deep, but it also hardened me. I walked away knowing I could never again put blind faith in a system that valued power over integrity.

After Novara, I was only unemployed for about two weeks before the phone rang with a lifeline. It was Tim. He told me he had a position opening up and that it would give me growth. He said he knew the type of worker I had been at Novara, that he had seen my effort and my fight, and he wanted to give me a fair shot.

Tim sent me an email with the job description and even guided me on what to say during the interview. For the first time in months, I felt like someone believed in me again.

When it came time to interview at StellarGen Research Facility, I sat across from Zhi. He was a handsome Asian man in his early forties, sharp and confident. During the interview, he made it clear I was butchering my own story — all the things I could have said about my resume, I didn't. He pointed them out one by one, almost like he was teaching me how to see myself differently. Toward the end, he admitted he didn't have much weight in the hiring process, but his honesty stuck with me.

The final interview was with his boss, Diane. Tim had given me advice before I walked in, and it helped steady me. Diane had also worked at Novara, so we immediately connected over the horrors of that place. We laughed a little, sharing stories, shaking our heads at the madness we had both endured. She was personable, down-to-earth, and though she carried a bit of a tomboyish edge, she radiated warmth. In her fifties, she seemed seasoned, grounded, and real.

A few days after my call with Diane, the offer came. Another 10% increase from what I had been making at Novara. A hybrid schedule, with the understanding that if I needed to work from home because of the kids, they would support me. Zhi told me plainly: *"I don't care why you go, when you go, or how you go. I just care that your work is done."* It was the kind of freedom I had been craving.

8

Balancing Act

The best part about starting at StellarGen Research Facility
was discovering that Trina had also left Novara and was now
working there too. We were reunited, this time on different
sides of Quality — she was in Supplier Quality, and I was in
QMS Quality. Seeing her again felt like a victory in itself. We
had survived Laurie's chaos together, and now here we were,
building something new in a healthier environment. Having her
nearby gave me comfort, a reminder that I wasn't alone in this
journey which was great because the first month at StellarGen
Research Facility was brutal. I had no idea about systems,
system management, or configurations. Quality Assurance was
foreign territory. I felt like I was drowning in acronyms and
procedures, every day a new wave crashing over me. Zhi was
not much help when it came to training. Still, I refused to give
up. I stayed up all night, night after night, learning the system
by playing in a sandbox environment where I had owner rights.
I broke things, fixed them, tested them, and learned by trial
and error.

In Quality Assurance, I quickly grasped the fundamentals of

document control. I understood the importance of precision —
making sure every record was documented clearly, consistently,
and correctly. It wasn't just about filing paperwork; it was
about creating a trail of accountability, ensuring that every step
could be traced, verified, and trusted. Those basics became the
foundation I leaned on while I struggled to master the more
complex systems.

As the weeks went on, I moved beyond just understanding
document control. I began learning how to configure the quality
systems themselves. At first, the screens and options felt
overwhelming, but little by little I pieced them together. I
taught myself how to create new workflows — mapping out
each step so that documents moved through the right chan-
nels, approvals were captured, and nothing slipped through
the cracks. I learned how to manage users and user groups,
assigning roles and responsibilities so that the system reflected
the structure of the company.

Metadata became another layer I had to master. I figured
out how to add new fields and categories, tailoring the system
so that information could be tracked more efficiently. Each
adjustment made the system stronger, more reliable, and easier
to navigate.

Security was the most critical piece. I realized that if users had
too much freedom, the integrity of document control could be
compromised. So I learned how to configure rights — removing
the ability to delete, restricting edits, and tightening permis-
sions so that the quality system stayed safe. Every safeguard I
put in place was designed to protect against deviation, to ensure
that records remained accurate and untouchable.

Through it all, I actually felt good about learning. For the
first time in years, the possibilities for growth seemed endless.

Every challenge pushed me harder, and instead of breaking me, it fueled me. Zhi had a way of throwing me straight into the fire, forcing me to figure things out on my own. And strangely, that's what gave me freedom. He granted me the same system rights he had — not because he wanted to mentor me, but because he was lazy. His only real concern was having his cup of coffee, black, while sitting back and watching me work. He even admitted it.

Zhi would monitor how long it took me to complete tasks, making sure I was never not busy. He had me completing his weekly reports, the ones he was supposed to send to his boss. But the truth was, all the things I put in those reports were tasks I was actually completing myself. Zhi really had it made, and he let everyone know it.

The irony was that his laziness became my opportunity. With full system rights, I could dive deeper than most people ever got the chance to. I learned how to configure workflows from scratch, manage user groups, add metadata, and lock down security features to protect document integrity. There were times when the system broke in ways Zhi didn't understand, and he'd sit back with his black coffee while I figured it out. The first time I solved a major configuration issue that had stalled the team for days, I realized I had surpassed him.

My boss wasn't the greatest teacher, but he gave me something more valuable: freedom. Freedom to learn if I put in the effort. And I did. Every late night, every mistake corrected, every small victory truly built me up.

But growth at work didn't mean life slowed down at home. I was still taking care of the kids — making dinner, keeping up with the housework, cleaning, and trying to hold everything together. The hybrid schedule gave me flexibility, but it also meant I was constantly juggling: logging off from a long day of training only to step right into laundry, dishes, homework, and bedtime routines.

Around this time, Miguel continued to show no desire for growth. He put in the bare minimum when it came to contributing to the house, especially after I had started that first biotech job at Novara. His lack of ambition weighed heavily on me, yet I still wanted us to work. I wanted my family intact, not fractured like the broken homes I came from. So I kept trying—carrying the weight, convincing myself that if I shouldered enough responsibility, maybe we could still stand strong together.

But I wasn't perfect either. After Miguel's betrayal, I felt disconnected, hollow in ways I couldn't explain. Shannon's betrayal had already left scars, and somewhere in the aftermath I started leaning into tattoos as a way to cope. The artist had been in my life since my very first tattoo, and after Shannon I found myself going back more often, adding ink to my skin as if each piece could stitch me back together.

Miguel and I were not great. I told him I wanted a divorce over and over, crying for hours just to get his attention, and he gave me nothing. It took me telling him I wanted to fuck my tattoo artist to finally spark a reaction. He left for a few days, and in that space I chose to do exactly what I had threatened—I slept with the artist. The irony was cruel: he wanted me too, but when the moment came, he couldn't get it up. Limp dick, wasted night.

Miguel came back begging for us to work it out again, and so we did. For a short time, it felt like maybe we were trying again, but the cracks were still there.

At one point, we even tried couples therapy. It lasted a few months with a man named David, whose home doubled as his office. Each session, Miguel and I sat together on a couch in David's cozy little house while he perched on a loveseat nearby. He'd peel off his socks and shoes, then rest his bare feet on the chair beside me—so close they nearly touched my arm. Old man feet, right in my space. It was gross, distracting, and impossible to ignore. For a short while, Miguel and I bonded over the absurdity of it, laughing about the stinky therapist's feet and the basil David insisted on feeding us for whatever reason. We thought maybe we were getting better, maybe the effort was paying off. But it wasn't. The feet were too much, the therapy too strange, and when we stopped going, Miguel stopped trying altogether. That was when his effort dropped to zero.

The exhaustion was relentless, pressing down on me day after day. There were nights when I could barely keep my eyes open, yet I reminded myself it would pay off later. I told myself over and over: I need to do this for my kids. They were my reason, my anchor. If I succeeded, they would see what was possible. If I kept pushing, they would know that strength and perseverance could carry them too. Every sacrifice, every late night, every moment of fatigue became a promise—that my hard work now would open doors for them in the future.

And despite the exhaustion, the pride was real. Each small victory at StellarGen Research reminded me that I was capable of more than anyone had ever given me credit for. I wasn't just building a career—I was shaping a version of myself that was stronger, sharper, and unwilling to be erased.

StellarGen Research wasn't perfect, but it was different. It gave me room to prove myself, and slowly I began to see the results of all the effort I had poured in. For the first time in a long time, I felt like I wasn't just surviving—I was growing.

9

The Summit

After my first year at StellarGen, the recognition came. They gave me another 10% raise and a $10,000 year-end bonus. For a start-up pharmaceutical company, the perks were incredible. My health insurance and deductible were fully covered. Even my electric bill and phone bill were paid by the company since I sometimes worked from home. It felt like weight was being lifted off my shoulders piece by piece. For the first time, I wasn't constantly worrying about how to stretch every dollar.

That was when I really started to care less about what Miguel was doing or how much he was making. As long as I could earn enough and provide for the kids, that was all that mattered. StellarGen Research gave me the independence I had been craving, and with each paycheck and perk, the weight of relying on him lifted off my shoulders.

My boss and I grew close during that year. Daily lunches became our routine. Sometimes it was just the two of us, sometimes Trina joined, and occasionally Tim came along. We'd head to the Brazilian café, order food, and sip fruity alcoholic drinks before heading back to work for the last few hours of the day. StellarGen Research wasn't strict — they even kept alcohol stocked in the fridge, mostly wine and White Claws, free for anyone to grab.

One time Zhi had an interview scheduled. He didn't drink much, but he opened the fridge and accidentally grabbed a White Claw, mistaking it for Pepsi. I thought it was hilarious. He didn't.

Diane often called us the "dynamic duo." Whatever Zhi said went, and I always followed through. I watched him attend a Validis Systems summit during my first year, and as the second year approached, he made sure I knew to plan ahead. Zhi and I became very close in that first year.

It was a platonic relationship, but the tension between us was undeniable. Every time we were together, I could feel it. I knew that if I ever initiated something, we would have crossed a line — breaking the vows we had made to our spouses. I never allowed myself to go there. My last boss at Novara had taught me a hard lesson: management will always come before the so-called "lower class peasants" in the company. That lesson stayed with me. I knew I had to tread lightly, to keep things professional even when the air between us felt charged. That's what we both wanted — to keep the line intact. And yet, when the time for the summit came, everything between us shifted.

I remember one time he told me not to message him after hours. I agreed, but that same night he messaged me at 8 p.m. Sometimes we'd hop on Teams calls late at night. He'd pretend to watch the work I was doing, but really we were just talking nonsense. His humor was one of a kind. Everyone at work seemed fearful of him, yet I only saw the light in him. Sure, I never knew when he was being serious or joking, but that unpredictability made him even more special.

Zhi was handsome, and he knew it. He'd tell everyone he was beautiful, even calling himself Mariah Carey. His charisma was magnetic — the kind of energy that filled a room. One year, I bought him a mug that said, *"My spirit animal is Mariah Carey."* He wasn't gay or anything — it was just his personality, his flair, that made him stand out.

As the summit approached again, I booked my trip well in advance. At home, I prepared with Miguel to make sure the kids had everything they needed while I was gone. I wanted to be fully present for the summit, knowing how much Zhi expected me to plan ahead and how much I had already grown in my role.

The day of the summit was nothing like I had imagined. Zhi didn't come on site that morning and went stone-silent the entire day, even when it was time for me to leave the office and head to Boston. The silence felt heavy, deliberate. I could sense something was off even the day before — like he was carrying someone else's frustration that had spilled over onto him.

Zhi never talked much about his wife or kids. I had met her once at the Christmas party the year before, and she looked tired, worn down, like the weight of something heavy was pressing on her. She hadn't left Zhi's side that whole night. Whenever someone tried to strike up a conversation with her, the responses were short, almost guarded. It was as if she wanted to make sure no one got too close, or maybe to remind him that she was always watching.

Zhi had made comments before, saying his wife hated him. He'd say it to another employee with me present, almost as if he wanted me to hear it. I couldn't shake the thought that maybe she had found out I was going to the summit. Maybe that explained the sudden shift, the distance he put between us. I felt strongly that he was treating me differently because I was a woman — that his wife didn't like me and had told him to stay away. But that didn't make it right. It was discriminatory.

The worst part was how little I knew about what to actually do once I got to Boston. I had no idea which seminars I was supposed to attend, where I was supposed to meet up with Zhi, or even how the schedule worked. He had gone stone-silent the day before, and that silence carried into the summit itself. There was no guidance, no plan laid out for me, just a vague expectation that I would somehow figure it out.

Walking into the summit felt overwhelming. Rooms filled with professionals who seemed to know exactly where they were going, which sessions mattered, and who they needed to connect with. Meanwhile, I was left standing there, unsure of where to start.

That's why I knew he was purposely ignoring me. He understood how much guidance I needed that day — the schedule, the seminars, the logistics of the summit — and yet he stayed silent. For all the times he had let me figure things out on my own, this was different. This was the one thing he had promised he would attend with me, the one time I expected him to step in and lead.

Instead, I watched him guide Ravi— a male colleague, the same employee he had once mocked and dismissed. Zhi showed him which rooms to go to, who to speak with, even where to eat. He gave Ravi the exact guidance I had begged for, while his only direct employee — me — was told to "go away." The betrayal cut deeper than anything before.

I couldn't hold it in anymore. During the summit, I called Trina, my voice shaking as I complained about Zhi and how upset I was. I cried on the phone because the anxiety was crushing me — I didn't know where to go, which seminars to attend, or how to navigate any of it. I told her how I had finally seen Zhi, but instead of helping me, he was with Ravi.

And when I finally saw Zhi face-to-face, he threw his bag over his shoulder and said, "Get away, Aurora." Hundreds of people surrounded me, none of whom I knew, and he walked straight into a seminar without another word. Because he told me to get away, I didn't follow him. Instead, I attended a different session — one that turned out to be useless for me. It was basic material, things I had already mastered long ago. I sat there, frustrated and upset, knowing I was wasting my time. Later, I vented to Trina again, telling her everything.

The second night brought an evening event that felt surreal. Clouds floated across the ceiling, women dressed in bright orange flight-attendant outfits carried drinks, and performers spun on poles, flipping through the air. It was extravagant, almost dreamlike, but I felt out of place.

That's when I spotted Celia from StellarGen. Everyone called her Cece, and the name fit her—this radiant sixty-seven-year-old woman with short, neck-length, voluminous tight curls that bounced with every confident step. She carried herself like someone who'd earned her place in every room, yet what I loved most was how unfailingly sweet she always was. As the VP of Clinical, she'd taken a real liking to me during the months we spent integrating her departments documents into our system—rewriting her procedures, cleaning up the formatting and, as an administrator, I was able to fast track documents in the system to approval with efficiency. That work built a quiet trust between us, and seeing Cece there felt like a small gift in the middle of all the chaos. Cece lit up the moment she saw me and gave me a hug. She told me later that she'd only come for the evening party, but the second she spotted Zhi and Ravi, she practically herded us together.

Zhi wouldn't tell her no. Instead, he waited until Cece and Ravi left to get drinks, then leaned toward me and asked how my days had been. I told him the truth — that I had no idea what I was doing, that I was upset with him, and that I had received zero guidance. His response cut deep: "Don't worry, you'll be gone soon enough."

To me, it felt like a threat. His tone carried something sharp, something final. I walked out, shaken, and that's when I met Kelvin. He was the director of cloud services, professional but slightly flirty, and he invited me to the after-after party. For a moment, I felt seen, like someone was acknowledging me.

But then Zhi appeared. He walked down just as Kelvin was inviting me, and before I could even respond, Zhi stepped in and said, "You should probably leave." Kelvin noticed it immediately — the jealousy in Zhi's eyes. He didn't push, but the tension was obvious.

I didn't want to make things worse. So instead of joining Kelvin, I went back to my room. Alone, I cried all night.

The last day of the summit was a haze. I walked into the first seminar I could find, sat quietly, and tried to absorb whatever I could. Some of the sessions gave me bits of knowledge, but most of the ones I chose weren't designed for my role or the purpose I was supposed to be there for. I felt like I was drifting, just moving from room to room without direction, trying to make sense of it all.

By then, all I wanted was to go home. To be with my kids. To leave behind the silence, the rejection, and the constant feeling of being out of place. I was miserable, sitting in rooms that didn't fit me, surrounded by strangers, knowing that the person who should have been guiding me had chosen to ignore me instead.

Before I knew it, the summit was over. The lights dimmed, the crowds thinned, and I was heading back home. What should have been an empowering experience ended as a hollow one — a haze of sessions that didn't fit, silence where there should have been support, and the sinking realization that I had been left to navigate it all alone.

The summit had become everything I hadn't expected — not a celebration of growth, but the turning point. Everything that had once felt beautiful about StellarGen Research was suddenly exposed as a lie. And for the first time, I understood: Zhi's treatment of me wasn't about guidance or leadership. It was discrimination — against me, for being female, while a male colleague received the support I had been denied.

10

Aisle 4

I remember the times Zhi and I would joke about who would be next in the "unemployment aisle 4 line." It was dark humor, but it was our way of acknowledging his history of getting rid of employees he didn't like. What I never realized was that, even for no real rhyme or reason, he would eventually do the same to me.

The day after the summit, we returned to work. I went straight to HR and complained about what had happened. I knew if it wasn't documented, he could twist things. I already had trust issues from everything in my life that had occurred, so I had to protect myself by putting it on record. As much as I hoped he just needed a better night's sleep, I wanted to believe that when we returned to the office, we'd fall back into our usual rhythm.

But that hope disappeared the moment I walked back on site. The first task he gave me was to complete a form to remove almost all of my rights to the system. When I asked why he was doing this, he simply said, "Complete the form." He wouldn't even do it himself — he made me request the removal of my own access.

From there, the humiliation only grew. For weeks, he gave me tasks and then changed the directions after I completed them. It reminded me of Laurie, but worse, because I had admired him once. He monitored every task I finished, only to hand me a whole different set of instructions afterward. It was a cycle designed to make me look incompetent.

I documented everything. I pulled audit trails for each task I completed, determined to show his boss, Diane, what was happening. Deep down, I believed the company wanted to do the right thing, and what Zhi was doing to me made no sense. Instead, we ended up in weekly meetings with him, Diane, and me, discussing how we could "overcome this." But there was no overcoming it. He wasn't trying to fix anything — he was dismantling my job functions piece by piece, trying to make me look bad.

He became malicious because I had reported the way he treated me at the summit. Even HR agreed that what he was doing was wrong. And then, HR was gone. Fired.

One day, after hours of back-and-forth nonsense tasks and a pretend meeting he scheduled to demote me from my role, I reached my breaking point. He claimed I wasn't completing tasks, that I was inefficient, and demanded I sign a new job description accepting a lower-level role. There was no HR present. I refused to sign and walked out.

That night, I sent audit trails, proof of the discrepancies in all of his messages. I proved what was going on. And the end result? At 5 p.m., I got an email from Diane saying she, Zhi, and I would have a chat the next morning.

I remembered Novara Biopharma and what they had told me previously — how it was "for a new role" and to come on site. I knew exactly what they were about to do. I was being fired.

By then, I was emotionally exhausted. I felt defeated. I had once admired Zhi, and now it felt like the ultimate betrayal. The person I had trusted most had turned against me, dismantling my role piece by piece.

So instead of going in the next morning, I went to my doctor. I told her everything, broke down, and cried. She listened, and then she put me on paid medical leave — a place where, at least for the moment, I couldn't be fired.

When I stepped away on medical leave, the weight of everything finally hit me. I had implemented three quality systems in a little over a year — endless sleepless nights, pouring myself into the work, sacrificing time with my kids, all because I wanted to prove myself. I wanted my family to see that I was capable, that I had talent, that I could build something meaningful.

But in that moment, it felt like it had all washed away. All the dedication, all the nights I stayed up working, all the effort I put into StellarGen — gone. I felt like nothing. No one. As if I had no talent all over again.

The exhaustion wasn't from the work; it was from Zhi. He had once been someone I admired, someone I thought respected me. To have him turn on me, to strip away my role and humiliate me, felt like the ultimate betrayal. And Trina, who had known everything, who had been my confidante, went silent the moment I took leave. She chose to protect herself and her job instead of standing by me.

She had become my best friend, or at least I thought she had. But when the time came, she chose to protect herself and her job rather than speak the truth about what was going on. That silence cut deep. Her silence cut almost as deep as Zhi's stab in the back. If the friendship had been mutual, she wouldn't have gone radio silent on me the moment I took my leave. I was left alone, carrying the weight of everything, with no ally to lean on.

Medical leave gave me space, but it never gave me peace. I was broken, exhausted, and grieving the loss of everything I had built. What should have been a career milestone — implementing three quality systems in just over a year — now felt meaningless. Instead of pride, I was left with emptiness.

My weeks filled with therapy sessions. Sometimes once a week, sometimes twice. I would sit across from a therapist and cry, pouring out the same questions again and again: *Why did Zhi do this? How could he turn on me? How could someone I was so close to suddenly treat me like I was nothing?*

It didn't make sense. I replayed every moment, every conversation, every decision, searching for answers that never came. I thought if I could just understand the reason, it would hurt less. But the truth was, it didn't matter why. What mattered was what I did now. That was the hardest lesson to face — that closure might never come, and I had to move forward without it.

Opening up to a therapist was its own battle. After everything I had endured, trusting someone enough to share my pain felt almost impossible. But the weight was too heavy to carry alone. Each session was raw, exposing wounds I had tried to hide, admitting how broken I felt, how betrayed I had been.

And while I was trying to heal, things at home were unraveling too. Miguel's anger was constant. He blamed me for everything — for the problems with Zhi, for losing my job, for the instability that followed. He accused me of cheating, twisting my pain into something ugly that wasn't true. Every day he told me I was lazy, that I couldn't do anything right. His words cut deeper than I could explain. I had already lost my career, my confidence, my sense of worth. Now, at home, I was being told I was worthless too. The loneliness was sharp — he had stopped sharing a bed with me, and the physical separation only deepened the emotional one.

I thought medical leave meant protection. I thought the laws in place would shield me. But protection turned out to be a thin line — one that could be bent, broken, and covered up like the rest of their document control messes.

A month into my leave, texts began to arrive from colleagues. They said they couldn't believe what had happened, that they would miss me. Confused, I asked what they meant. That's when they told me: I had been let go.

How could that be? I was still on medical leave. But it turns out they *can* do it — and they did. The company fired me and sent an email the following week, after the news had already been broadcasted to everyone else.

I really was now in unemployment aisle 4. The joke Zhi and I used to share had become my reality. Without Tim, without Trina, without anyone I "knew" to help me back into the field, I was lost. It was starting from scratch.

I knew I had to gain control back. I couldn't stay in that place of defeat. So I started applying for jobs — everywhere. Every single day, I sent out at least five applications. Even jobs I didn't want, I applied to. It didn't matter, as long as they were within the same industry. I didn't care about dipping my toes into something new; I just needed stability again. For my kids. For me. For the sake of my marriage.

The months dragged on. Rejection emails piled up, silence followed most applications, and the weight of uncertainty pressed harder each day. Miguel's anger didn't let up. His accusations echoed in my head even as I tried to focus on rebuilding.

I felt trapped, but I knew I couldn't stay there. I had to claw my way back, to prove to myself that I wasn't broken, that I still had worth. I had implemented three quality systems in just over a year, poured myself into sleepless nights, sacrificed so much — and yet it felt like all of it had been erased. I was determined to show that it hadn't been for nothing.

Finally, after months of searching, I caught a break. Aureflex called me back for a third interview. The process was long, and the pay was less than I had hoped, but the role was familiar — QMS and document control. It was something I knew, something I could build on. For the first time in months, I felt a flicker of hope.

11

New beginnings

Walking into Aureflex felt like stepping into another universe compared to my last two positions. The culture was younger, less experienced, and far less compliant. It wasn't pharmaceuticals — it was medical devices — but even so, the gaps were glaring.

I noticed them almost immediately. Document management was scattered, processes were inconsistent, and compliance seemed more like an afterthought than a requirement. During my first week, I was assigned training documents in the ComplianceWire system. By the second procedure, I realized something shocking: they had three separate QMS systems in place. Three. The goal is always one unified system, so how did they end up with three? Their procedures weren't easy to follow either. If my twelve-year-old daughter had walked in, she probably could have written them better.

As I dug deeper, the cracks widened. Most employees didn't even know the difference between a procedure and a work instruction. Some didn't know what GMP stood for. When I asked Adriana, the girl training me, she shrugged and said, "We don't do that here." I laughed to myself at the absurdity. *You don't do that here?* In order to sell medical devices, compliance with GMP standards isn't optional — it's the law.

And that's when I realized: this was where I could make a real difference. Fixing their document management, streamlining their processes, teaching them compliance — that would be my superpower here.

What struck me most was the irony. I had only two and a half years of experience in pharmaceuticals, yet the knowledge I carried outshone people who had been at Aureflex for years. Funnier still, I had no college degree, yet I held more credible information on how to make small changes that led to big impacts — saving time, strengthening compliance, and , proving my worth.

My cubicle neighbor, Baihan, picked up on my work style early. He was something Middle Eastern, skinny, average height, with great hair he clearly treated like a personality trait. Brilliant in that nerdy, effortlessly confident way — the kind of guy who could get away with anything because everyone knew he was too smart to fail.

I remember he had all three of his monitors open, *all of them* playing Minecraft — not even pretending to hide it — and he still finished his tasks faster than the rest of us combined. It was ridiculous, and honestly, hilarious.

We first bonded over music. He kept trying to make conversation with me, asking random questions just to get me talking. I remember he asked what I listened to, and when I said *Sticky Fingers*, he laughed and called me a little hippie. It was stupid and funny and somehow exactly what I needed.

But beneath that small pocket of levity, I came with baggage, of course. Two kids at home. A broken husband who barely spoke to me anymore. But I stood my ground. I leveraged the knowledge I had gained from my last two companies, and slowly, I built the confidence to hold my place.

At the same time, I was still fighting another battle. I was suing my last company for firing me while on medical leave. I went through the state and blew the whistle. I didn't care. They needed to be held accountable. A man fighting with his wife shouldn't mean I lose my job for calling him out on suddenly treating me differently because I was a woman. I fought hard, even as my marriage continued to fail. Miguel and I still slept in different rooms, barely speaking. I chose silence over the constant fights, over the endless accusations that I couldn't do anything right for our family.

But at Aureflex, I wore a mask. To the new employees, I lied about my life. I told them I was happily married, that my family was beautiful, that I had only lost my last role due to unforeseen circumstances when the company had to let go of many employees. It was easier to paint a picture of stability than to reveal the chaos I was living in. They didn't need to know the truth — that my marriage was cumbling, that I had been singled out and fired unfairly, that I was still clawing my way back.

As I was settling in, I met another colleague. His name was Matthew, and he was impossible to ignore—his skin reminded me of the drink I loved, warm and rich with a caramel swirl. He was undeniably attractive, the kind of man whose cologne reached me across the building before he did.

He sat just behind me, and from the start I could feel the heat of his stare even before I knew him. Whenever I turned my head to glance back, he'd whip his eyes away so fast it was almost comical—like he hadn't just been staring, like he hadn't been caught admiring me. The speed of it only confirmed what I already felt.

On the second day, he waited until everyone else had left before approaching me. "Has anyone given you a tour yet?" he asked. I shrugged, "Kinda, not really." That was all he needed— he wanted to show me around. And maybe, deep down, he just wanted my attention.

He walked me through the building, introducing me to more colleagues, pointing out spaces I hadn't seen yet. The whole time, his scent lingered—clean, warm, intoxicating—and it was hard not to look at him, hard not to ignore the pull. I was married, and so everything I felt in those moments stayed locked inside my head. They were just thoughts, nothing more. I played it safe, kept my distance, and let the attraction live quietly in the background.

Then he showed me our so-called "clean room," which didn't really exist. Instead, the company used grow tents for certain validation projects—literally marijuana grow tents repurposed for sterilizing medical devices or other nature-related work. It was absurd and hilarious, and I couldn't help but laugh at the thought of medical validation happening inside something meant for cultivating weed. The way he grinned when I laughed only made it harder to resist him.

When I stayed late that first week, he'd play music that felt like a secret message. One night it was *"Lovin on Me"* by Jack Harlow, pulsing through the quiet office like a confession wrapped in rhythm. I was subtly sure it was meant for me, like he wanted to whip that "lovin on me" energy straight in my direction without ever saying it. I knew, but I kept my back turned, pretending not to notice, pretending not to care.

It didn't take long before Matthew asked me to join him and

a group of coworkers for drinks to welcome me. I knew from experience that going out was the way "in," the unspoken rule of fitting into a new workplace. I said yes. Not just because it was the way "in," but because I needed a reprieve. I needed to breathe outside the suffocating walls of my home. I needed to remember what it felt like to feel alive, even if it was only temporarily. So the next day I went out for drinks.

Walking into the bar, I felt like I was stepping onto a stage. My smile was rehearsed, my laugh carefully timed, my posture straightened to project confidence I didn't feel.

I had to become someone else that night. Someone fun, someone intelligent, someone lighthearted. I had to pretend that nothing else was going on in my life—that the lawsuits, the betrayals, the unemployment, the broken friendships weren't weighing me down. I had to smile like I hadn't cried in the car on the way there. I had to laugh like my chest wasn't tight with anxiety, even though every breath felt like it carried the weight of everything I was trying to hide.

Jake n Joe's was buzzing already, the kind of suburban bar where the lights are dim but the chatter is loud, where televisions glow with sports highlights and the smell of fried food clings to the air. I tried to carry myself like I belonged, like I was just another person out for a casual night, not someone dragging invisible baggage behind her.

The first test of my disguise came quickly. The waitress, young and sharp-eyed, asked for my ID. I handed her my expired license, hoping she wouldn't notice. She did. I tried my birth certificate, then my social security card, fumbling through documents that proved who I was but not in the way she needed. She shook her head firmly, refusing them all. For a moment, embarrassment burned hot in my chest. I felt exposed, like the mask I had worked so hard to wear was slipping.

Luckily, Matthew showed up and spared me from the worst of the embarrassment. He leaned in, casual and confident, and offered a solution. "Come on," he said, gesturing toward the door. Outside, in his car, he handed me little bottles—shots of Fireball whiskey. The cinnamon burn was sharp, but it dulled the sting of humiliation. We laughed together, the kind of laughter that comes from shared mischief, from bending the rules just enough to feel alive.

We even went for a quick ride down the street to the liquor store before everyone showed up at the bar, his music low in the background, the night air cool against my skin. He picked up what we needed without hesitation, moving through the errand like it was nothing. On the way back, he glanced at me and said, almost offhandedly, "You remind me of an ex. Not in a bad way."

To me, that was weird—an odd compliment wrapped in comparison—but I shrugged it off. *Whatever,* I thought. I wasn't there to be anyone's reminder of the past. I was there to survive the thrive in the present, to prove to myself that I could still show up, still laugh, still pretend to be the kind of person who fit in. I went on to tell him that he looked dangerous, like someone I wouldn't dare be alone with. As we were pulling back into the parking lot I made another joke to him saying he looks like the kind of guy that listens to Chris brown. He laughed and admitted that was true.

Back at the bar I shook hands, exchanged pleasantries, and pretended that I wasn't terrified of being judged. I told myself to be compassionate, to be warm, to show strength—even if it was only borrowed strength, borrowed peace. Later, the we would all laugh about it—the absurdity of me trying to prove my age with a stack of papers that belonged in a filing cabinet, not a bar. The waitress even cracked a smile when she realized I wasn't angry, just mortified. It became a running joke for the evening, a small thread of humor woven into the night.

And so I kept playing the role. Fun. Intelligent. Lighthearted. The woman who could laugh at ID mishaps, who could sip Fireball in a stranger's car, who could smile through the ache in her chest. Pretending wasn't just about fooling them—it was about fooling myself, about creating a version of me that felt strong enough to carry the night.

That night, I became the version of myself people wanted to be around. The one who could tell stories, make jokes, ask thoughtful questions. The one who seemed like she had it all together. I knew how to play that role—I had rehearsed it for years.

But it was exhausting. Every laugh felt like a lie. Every smile felt like a mask. I wanted them to see me as fun and intelligent, not broken and weary. I wanted them to believe I was strong, even when I felt like I was crumbling. I didn't want anyone to know my pains—the nights I lay awake, jaw clenched, replaying betrayals. The fear that unemployment might return, that stability was always temporary. The scars left by my past.

So I pretended. I pretended to be the person I thought they wanted. And in that pretending, I found a strange kind of strength. Because sometimes, pretending is the only way to survive.

I made a few acquaintances that night. Some faces blurred together, but others stood out—people who seemed genuine, who asked questions about my life without judgment. For a moment, I thought I could see myself forming good friendships with most of them. It was fragile hope, but it was hope nonetheless.

One encounter in particular still makes me smile. As we were talking, I realized I actually knew one of the men from years earlier, though not in the way most people meet. Funny enough, I had drawn his blood back when I was working at QuantumCore Laboratories . Without thinking about HIPAA or the awkwardness of bringing up something so personal, I blurted out: "Hey didnt I use to draw your blood?"

He laughed, not offended at all, and admitted he remembered the visits. I hadn't realized he was part of the welcoming group that night, so I then got curious and asked why he was there. The surprise came when I learned he wasn't just another friendly face—he was the Director of Product Development. The kind of person whose name carried weight in meetings, whose decisions shaped entire projects.

Instead of being put off by my comment, he found it funny, even interesting. He joked about how small the world was, how strange it felt to meet someone in one context and then again in such a different one. His kindness put me at ease, and for the first time that evening, I felt like maybe I wasn't just pretending to belong. Maybe I really could.

But the night didn't end there.

Hours later, I stumbled toward my car, the alcohol heavy in my veins. Matthew walked beside me, steady, protective, his presence impossible to ignore. When we reached my car, he looked at me with eyes I'll never forget—eyes that said *mine*. It was indescribable, the way he stared at me, like he wanted me, like he was about to take me even though I was married.

I had felt it the moment we met—that pull, that warning. Now, standing in the dark, his gaze confirmed it.

Instead, I forced myself to hold his stare, sharp as I could with drunken eyes, and whispered, "Have a good night." He buckled me in said "drive safe". He drove away, and I pretended to do the same. But I didn't. I stayed there, curled in my car, sleeping it off for three hours. I had kids to go home to, and I couldn't risk driving until I could at least steady myself. So I took a nap.

Looking back, I realize that night wasn't about drinks or acquaintances. It was about survival. It was about proving to myself that I could still show up, still connect, still find pieces of peace even when my heart was heavy. I wanted stability, and if I couldn't find it, I would create the illusion of it until it became real.

When I finally made it home though, I was still fuzzy. The morning after that night out was brutal. I dont know how I made it out of bed. I climbed into my Jeep to head to work—and projected vomit everywhere. I mean everywhere. The smell, the mess, the humiliation. My husband looked at me with disgust. He reluctantly let me borrow his car after I explained, desperate, "If I lose this job, there goes the mortgage payments."

So I rushed into work, leaving behind my vomit-filled Jeep, carrying the weight of shame and survival all over again.

I dragged myself into work, praying no one would notice how unsteady I was. My body felt heavy, my head pounding, the shame of the Jeep still lingering. That's when Matthew appeared, almost casually, with Liquid I.V. packets and a handful of snacks. He didn't make a big deal of it, didn't tease me about the mess I'd made of myself—just handed them over with a look that said *I've got you.*

Then, with that sly grin of his, he held up a bottle of Fireball as the "alternate option." It was ridiculous, like offering me life in one hand and death in the other. "Hydrate... or die trying," his smirk seemed to say. Who does that? The contrast was so absurd it made me laugh, even through the pounding in my head.

It was such a small gesture, but it carried weight. In that moment, I realized how much I needed someone to see me—not as broken, not as exhausted, but simply as human. Matthew's kindness, wrapped in humor, helped me get through that day, one sip and one bite at a time. And I knew, going forward, I'd never touch Fireball again.

It wasn't long before my new job began to see my strengths. I saw the gaps, the inefficiencies, the risks. Since their systems were messy, the processes scattered, and compliance felt more like a suggestion than a standard, I spoke up.

To my surprise, they listened. Sahani, my boss, didn't dismiss me or tell me to stay quiet. Instead, she leaned in. She agreed to let me initiate making smaller changes at the site level, careful not to disrupt global processes. It was a chance to prove myself, to show that the knowledge I carried wasn't just theory—it could make a real difference.

When she invited me to the Validis Systems Summit that early on, it felt like validation. I wasn't just surviving anymore; I was being trusted to represent, to learn, to bring back ideas that could reshape the way we worked.

Everything seemed like it was finally starting to fall into place. At work, I was being recognized for my strengths, trusted to make changes. At home, my kids were just about finishing summer camp and preparing for the new school year. I threw myself into school shopping, determined to give them everything they needed for a fresh start—new clothes, crisp notebooks, sturdy backpacks, headphones, even the little accessories they begged for. I wanted them to feel ready, to feel secure, to feel like life was steady even if I was still piecing myself together.

It was the week before school started. I was driving home from work, the car humming beneath me, my mind already running through dinner plans and bedtime routines, when my phone rang. Miguel's name lit up the screen.

His voice was different—serious, quiet, almost rehearsed. "We need to talk," he said. "But I want to do it in person."

My chest tightened. "What are you talking about? What's going on?" I asked, my voice sharp with worry.

"I found a place," he said flatly. "I'm signing the papers today and moving out this weekend."

The words hit me like a blow. My heart dropped, my hands trembling against the steering wheel. Fifteen years together, and this was how it ended? No warning, no fight, no chance to fix it—just a phone call telling me he was gone.

I thought about all the weight I had carried—the bills, the groceries, the endless responsibilities of raising our children. I thought about the nights I stayed awake, wondering if we'd ever find our way back to each other. And now he was leaving me?

He said he couldn't take the distance in our relationship anymore, that he thought this was what was best for the kids. But in my mind, the words twisted into something darker: *he must have found someone younger, prettier again.*

Tears blurred my vision. I begged him to reconsider, asked if he wanted to at least make an in-law suite in the lower level of our home. A way to stay connected, to still be present for the kids without sharing the same space. He said no. His answer was final, cold.

Unless I begged him to stay—which I think was what he wanted, a way to keep control—he was leaving.

So I let him go.

The silence after that call was unbearable. The hum of the car felt louder, the road stretched endlessly before me, and all I could think was how fifteen years had dissolved into a single sentence. My chest ached, my throat burned, and I couldn't stop the tears from falling. I felt betrayed, abandoned, stripped of the fragile hope I had been clinging to.

That night, I sat alone in the quiet of the house, staring at the walls that had witnessed every fight, every laugh, every broken promise. The kids were asleep, their backpacks lined up neatly by the door, ready for school. And I wondered how I would tell them, how I would explain that their father had chosen to walk away and he's not coming back this time.

I had carried the weight for so long, but now it felt heavier than ever. The mortgage, the bills, the groceries, the endless responsibilities—all mine. And beneath it all, the echo of his words: *I'm moving out this weekend.*

That weekend, I did what I thought was best. I helped him pack. I gathered all his lingering clothes, washed them one last time, folded them neatly, and bagged them up for him. I wiped down the dressers, the TV stands, the living room furniture—every piece he decided was going with him. I let him take whatever he wanted.

There was no fight, no argument, no begging. I just wanted it to be done quietly, peacefully, without the kids watching their father walk out of our lives. My mom took them out for me, kept them busy, shielded them from the heaviness of that day.

The house felt hollow as I moved through it, preparing for his departure. Each drawer I emptied, each surface I cleaned, felt like erasing the traces of a life we had built together. Fifteen years reduced to bags of clothes and furniture carried out the door.

When he finally left, the silence was deafening. No more footsteps, no more angry voice echoing through the walls. No more holes being punched into our walls trying to break us down. Just me, standing in the stillness, knowing I had helped him walk out of our lives for the last time.

12

Friction and Friendship

The first few weeks after Miguel left were tough with the kids. They tested every ounce of my patience, pushing boundaries, acting out in ways I knew were rooted in hurt. Underneath their defiance, I could see it—they were grieving too. And I was hurting right alongside them. Juggling their emotions and mine felt impossible some days.

At work, I forced myself to hold a smile. I laughed at jokes, nodded through meetings, pretended everything was fine. Inside, I was crumbling. But I just wanted my kids to be happy. That was all that mattered.

It wasn't long before we all realized the truth. The moment he left, the house changed. There were no more wake-up calls of screaming. No more mean remarks cutting through the mornings and nights. It was just us three, and in that quiet, we found love again. I gave them extra affection, took them on long walks, kept the busy as to not fall apart the way I was.

At work, Matthew and the group we hung around with knew what was going on. I could only hide it for so long. Matthew especially wanted to step in and help. He offered to come by and put up the soccer net for my son—a promise Miguel had made before moving out but never kept, never came back to fulfill.

Matthew definitely wanted me. I could feel it in the way he looked at me, the way he lingered in conversations. And I liked the attention. It wasn't just attraction—it was the way he seemed to hear me without words, the way he could see my pain without me having to explain it.

So that weekend, Matthew and a couple of his buddies came by to set up the net. I thought it would be simple, but my mistake was not measuring the size beforehand. When they finished putting it together, I realized it was far too big for my yard. I asked them to take it down.

It could have been a moment of embarrassment, one where they laughed and called me crazy. But they didn't. They understood. They saw the size compared to the yard, and they respected my choice. I chose the yard over a giant net taking over the space.

In that moment, I realized something. It wasn't about the net—it was about being seen, about someone showing up when they didn't have to. Matthew's presence, his willingness to help, reminded me that even in the middle of heartbreak, there were still people willing to stand beside me.

Matthew filled a space I hadn't realized was empty. He offered help, small gestures that carried weight—like showing up with oranges or pineapples when I hadn't eaten, or checking in randomly when he knew the nights were heavy. He didn't need to say much; his presence was enough.

But with every glance, every subtle touch, the line between friendship and something more blurred. I had told him once that he looked dangerous, like someone I wouldn't dare be alone with. And yet, I felt the pull. His eyes carried a question I wasn't ready to answer, a claim I wasn't sure I could resist.

I was still married on paper, still healing from Miguel's departure, still trying to hold my children together. But Matthew's attention reminded me of something I hadn't felt in years—desire, possibility, the intoxicating rush of being wanted.

It was dangerous. It was tempting. It was exactly what I wasn't supposed to need.

However, it didn't take long before going out with Matthew and the Aureflex crew became a ritual. Every Friday, when the office let out early for "Flex Friday," we'd head straight to Jake n Joe's. It was our place—dim lights, high-top tables, the kind of bar where the regulars knew your name and the drinks came fast. For me, it was three hours of escape before I had to head home, three hours where I could laugh, sip a beer, and forget the heaviness still lingering behind my front door.

One Friday stands out more than the rest. I'd had two beers and a shot in that window of time—nothing outrageous, nothing I thought I couldn't handle. I felt fine, steady enough to drive. Later that evening, I swung by Taco Bell to pick up dinner for the kids. It was supposed to be quick, ordinary. But as I pulled out of the drive-through, I misjudged the turn and clipped the fire hydrant on my right side.

The sound was sharp—a pop that echoed in my chest. I kept driving, but the car dragged, heavy and uneven, the popped tire pulling me sideways. My stomach sank.

I called Miguel. Even though he had left, part of me still thought he might help. But his voice was cold, detached. "No, I don't have time," he said. "Try the neighbor. Maybe he'll help."

At first, I thought he was just being cruel, brushing me off. But I swallowed my pride and said, "Okay."

So I kept driving, the car limping along on its ruined tire. At a stoplight, a police cruiser pulled up beside me. The officer rolled down his window, leaned out, and asked, "Ma'am, are you aware you've got a problem?"

I looked at him, exhausted, embarrassed, and said with a half-laugh, half-snotty tone, "Yeah, I live right up that road. Did you want to follow me home?"

He chuckled, shaking his head. "No, looks like you've got it."

And just like that, he let me go. I drove the rest of the way home on a car that shouldn't have been moving, dragging myself and my mistakes back to the driveway.

When I finally pulled into the driveway, the car dragging on its ruined tire, I felt the weight of exhaustion pressing down on me. I knocked on my neighbor's door, hoping for help, but there was no answer. Out of desperation, I called Miguel. He said he'd reach out to the neighbor for me, his tone clipped, detached, as if this was just another inconvenience he couldn't be bothered with.

A few minutes later, I saw him. A man I had somehow never noticed before, though he lived right next door. He was tall, probably my age, with brown hair and soft hazel eyes that seemed to carry warmth. He walked over with a lift and a set of tools, moving with quiet confidence, like he had done this a hundred times before.

How had I never seen him? This was the neighbor whose son my boy went to play with, the man who had been living just steps away from me all this time. And yet, it felt like I was seeing him for the very first time.

He got to work quickly, no hesitation, no wasted motion. Within an hour, the tire was replaced, the car steady again, as if the whole ordeal had never happened. Watching him, I felt a strange mix of gratitude and curiosity.

I asked for his number, telling myself it was just to coordinate when my son went over to play with his. But deep down, I knew there was more to it. I wanted his number because I wanted to know him. *Who are you, and how have you been here this whole time without me noticing?*

Not long after, I offered beers one evening and stopped in. It was casual, neighborly, but beneath the surface, I felt the spark of something new—an opening, a possibility, a reminder that even in the middle of chaos, unexpected connections could appear right next door.

I quickly learned something about the neighbor that surprised me—he loved reading as much as I did. Books had always been my quiet refuge, though lately I hadn't had as much time to lose myself in them. Flex Fridays and my drinking splurges had stolen those hours, but still, it was comforting to see someone else light up over the same stories, the same authors, the same escape.

He was cool, easy to be around, the kind of person you could sit with in silence or talk with for hours without it ever feeling forced. There were no rules, no expectations. Just the unspoken understanding that we were both single neighbors, both carrying similar traumas, both raising boys the same age.

He liked books. I liked beer. Somehow, that balance worked. The boys would hang out together, running between yards, and I would too—sharing conversations with him that felt natural, effortless.

It didn't take long before he became one of my best friends. Not because we planned it, not because we tried, but because sometimes life places the right people beside you at the exact moment you need them most.

One night, as we sat talking, I mentioned my own little hobby—collecting rocks. It wasn't anything serious, just something I'd always found fascinating. I told him about one particular stone I had found, strange and unidentifiable. Curious, I had sent it off to a meteor guy for testing. He came back saying it was heavy in irons but carried so many different characteristics that he couldn't pin it down. In the end, he sent it back to me with the suggestion that I forward it to another lab for further analysis.

My neighbor listened with interest, then grinned. "Well, I've got a collection too," he said.

I raised an eyebrow, expecting something similar—maybe quartz, maybe fossils. Instead, he pulled out a box and revealed his collection: rocks shaped like cocks.

I couldn't help but laugh. It was hilarious, unexpected, and oddly endearing. Each stone had its own shape, its own personality, and yes—they all looked unmistakably like dicks.

It wasn't the same kind of collection as mine, but it was funny that he really collected them, proudly showing them off like treasures. There was something about the absurdity of it that broke the heaviness of the moment. We laughed together, the kind of laughter that comes from shared silliness, from realizing that sometimes life hands you humor in the strangest forms.

In that moment, I realized how easy it was to be around him. He wasn't trying to impress me, wasn't hiding behind walls. He was just himself—quirky, genuine, and unafraid to share the oddities that made him who he was. And I liked that.

From then on, we started playing the "hi neighbor" game. Anytime we saw each other — pulling into the driveway, step-ping outside, passing cars — we'd shout it. Hi neighbor! It became our thing. Our running joke. Our ritual.

And because I was the self-appointed author of our rulebook, I always got extra points. I always won. Even when he technically won, I'd make up a new rule so I still came out on top.

He'd just shake his head and laugh. I'd tell him to try harder next time.

Matthew was still on my mind. Even when I tried to focus on other things, he lingered there—his voice, his eyes, the way he seemed to pull me in without effort. I was still getting to know him, still piecing together who he really was.

Friends whispered that he was dating someone. That stung, so I asked him directly. When we first met, he had told me he'd just broken up with his girlfriend. Now his answer was different: she was still in the process of moving out, not someone he was dating anymore, just someone gathering her belongings. It was messy, but I wanted clarity because I could feel the tension between us growing stronger every day.

I started a book club at work, and Matthew joined. The first book we read together was *Atomic Habits.* There was a line about bumping and grinding until the friction came, and I couldn't resist—I sent Matthew a snippet of it. It was hot, suggestive, and I wanted him to know how I was feeling without saying it outright.

The next week, at book club, he read that entire passage out loud. My cheeks burned red, my pulse quickened, and just like that, I was turned on. It had been so long since I'd felt that kind of desire. Before Miguel left, a year had passed without intimacy, without touch, without passion. Matthew's voice reading that passage cracked something open inside me. I was at work, but my body betrayed me—heat rising, breath shallow, pants damp with longing.

A week later, the solar eclipse arrived. I had bought special glasses for my kids before heading into the office that morning. When the moment came, everyone stepped outside to watch the sky darken, the rare alignment unfolding above us. I stepped outside too, but not just for the eclipse—I needed air, needed space from the heat waves Matthew kept sending me. His subtle messages, his glances, his presence—it was overwhelming.

Whispers started circulating. People at work leaned in with warnings, their voices hushed but sharp. They said Matthew had slept with a lot of women there, that he had a history of manipulating, of playing with girls' heads. *Be careful,* they'd caution.

I didn't want to believe it. That couldn't be true—not with the way he looked at me, not with the way he made me feel seen. With him, it felt different. This was genuine. He wanted me, and I wanted him. I didn't care who he had been with before me, as long as he was honest about who he was now—while he was pulling me closer into his orbit.

Then one day, he messaged me: *Let me take you out.*

I teased back, *Sure... coffee?*

He laughed. *Yes.*

We met at Saki, just the two of us this time. No coworkers, no distractions, just him and me across the table. We laughed about the book club, about the red cheeks I couldn't hide when he read that passage aloud. We talked about our pasts—family, friendships, relationships that had soured. He told me he loved that I had kids, that he admired how much I poured into them, how I was such a good mom. His words made me feel good, seen in a way I hadn't felt in years.

When the check came, I reached for it, ready to see how much I should Venmo. He stopped me, his hand brushing mine, firm but gentle. *Not this time,* he said.

He walked me to my car afterward. Just as I was about to open the door, he stopped me—his hand on my arm, pulling me closer. And then he kissed me.

The kiss was electric, raw, like something ripped straight from a fantasy. His lips were soft, full, intoxicating. His hands caressed my body with a confidence that made me melt. If he had tried to fuck me right there in the parking lot, I would have let him. Desire surged through me, overwhelming, undeniable.

It had been so long since I'd felt that kind of passion. His kiss wasn't just a kiss—it was seduction, a reminder of everything I had been missing, everything I had been craving. The night ended with a kiss but I knew that was just the beginning.

13

Blurred Passion, Surfacing Lies

I was still hanging out with my neighbor daily, our boys running back and forth between yards while we sat outside talking. He was steady, easy, the kind of presence that made life feel lighter. We'd laugh about the small things that made the heaviness of life bearable. With him, there was no pressure, no games— just friendship and the comfort of knowing someone nearby understood.

The next few months blurred together in a haze. Matthew and I grew closer, carving out more time for ourselves during Flex Fridays. What started as casual drinks and laughter soon became something deeper, more dangerous. It wasn't long before I crossed the line with him.

I would sneak him into my home, quietly, carefully, making sure no one knew. Once the door closed behind us, we slipped into our own universe. We even gave names to the little rituals that stitched us together. I ate popcorn, he ate strawberries, and we shared oranges with our coffee and tea. He was my coffee— bold, waking, impossible to ignore—and the love we shared, we called Tea. We would spend the night together, tangled in passion, and somehow still managed to show up at work the next morning pretending nothing had happened. I don't know how we managed to function half the time. My body was exhausted, my mind foggy, but he was the best distraction I'd ever had.

He kept showing me effort—checking in, making me feel wanted—but there were cracks in his stories. Little inconsistencies that gnawed at me.

Months passed however, and somehow his ex was still living in his place. That unsettled me more than anything. It wasn't just about her—it was about honesty. I told him plainly, without hesitation: *I won't continue if she's still there.* The thought of being played, of being strung along while he lived a double life, made my stomach twist. I wasn't going to be part of that game.

I laid my frustration bare, told him how much it was wearing on me, how it made me question everything between us. He listened, and then one day at work, he came to me with a look of certainty. *She's gone for good,* he said. His words were firm, convincing, delivered with the kind of confidence that made me want to believe him. And so I did. I let myself breathe again, let myself fall deeper into the haze of us.

But the truth has a way of slipping through the cracks.

A few weeks later, we were out with friends, laughter spilling across the table, drinks in hand. That's when his buddy Baihan made the remark—casual, almost careless, but sharp enough to cut. It was so good to see Marina the other day at Matthew's house, he said. The words landed like a blow to the chest. My smile froze, my heart dropped. I knew Baihan meant it to dig at me, maybe even to expose something Matthew hadn't wanted me to know. But more than that, it revealed the truth: Matthew's lie. She wasn't gone. She had never been gone.

In that moment, the haze I had been living in—the passion, the secrecy, the intoxicating distraction—began to clear. And what was left was the sting from the stab in the back, sharp and undeniable.

Shortly after, I told Matthew I was done. Done with whatever situationship he had put me in, done with the half-truths and the inconsistencies. I tried to ignore him, to pull away, but he only tried harder to get me back.

Then one day at work, his other friend Tai approached me. His tone was softer, apologetic. He said she really was gone now, that Matthew hadn't told me because he was afraid I wouldn't understand. He didn't want to just kick her out, Tai explained, but it was over. He said Matthew truly wanted to try again with me, that if I still felt the way I did in the beginning, I should have faith it would all work out.

I listened, but it wasn't Tai's words that swayed me. It was my own heart. I wanted to believe. I wanted to believe that the passion I felt with Matthew couldn't be fake, that the intensity between us meant something real.

So I gave him another chance. Not because of Tai, not because of anyone else, but because I couldn't shake the hope that beneath the lies and the chaos, Matthew really did have feelings for me.

Sometime before Christmas, the whole office was carrying holiday energy vibes. The luncheon was filled with laughter, plates of food passed around, and the anticipation of Secret Santa gifts. Everyone joked about who had whose name, the small surprises wrapped in festive paper waiting to be opened.

When it was my turn, I didn't expect much—maybe a candle, maybe some chocolates. But Matthew had somehow convinced someone to give him my name. And when I opened the bag,

I realized he hadn't just picked something small. He had showered me in gifts.

He knew I liked crafting, so he bought epoxy, molds, and colors. He added snacks—bright oranges that reminded me of winter mornings, gloves to keep my hands warm, fuzzy socks soft enough to sink into, and then the sweater. A sweater that said *Coffee*. Coffee was my nickname for him, since that's how we started.

Out of all the Santa gifts received, mine was the largest, the most thoughtful, and probably the most expensive. He made me feel special, like I mattered, like he had gone out of his way to think about me.

In that moment, surrounded by coworkers and holiday cheer, I couldn't ignore the warmth that spread through me. His attention wasn't subtle anymore—it was deliberate, undeniable. And I let myself enjoy it, even if part of me knew it was dangerous to believe.

The Christmas party came not long after, hosted at Gillette Stadium in some fancy restaurant whose name I can't even remember. What I do remember is being there, surrounded by colleagues, the hum of conversation, the clinking of glasses, the kind of holiday cheer that feels both warm and exhausting.

My friend Ashira was there—HR by title, but more than that to me. She was beautiful, honest, raw. Confidence carried in every word she spoke. Dark skin glowing under the dim lights, big brown eyes that missed nothing, ethnic hair that framed her face like a crown. She had an attitude I wouldn't want to mess with, but that's what made her magnetic. She was my closest friend at Aureflex outside of Matthew, and I trusted her. Even though she was HR, I knew she could keep secrets. She was down to earth, the kind of person who could hold your truth without judgment.

Chris joined us too, another colleague who always brought easy laughter. Chris was a tall guy with ginger hair, I'd joke on how tall he was standing next to me since I'm barely five-foot.

The three of us claimed the dartboard, beers in hand, daring each other to play like pros. Shots lined up, one after another, and soon the warmth spread through me, the kind of buzz that makes everything funnier, lighter, easier.

I was losing terribly. My darts missed the mark more often than not, bouncing off the board or landing far from the bullseye. But instead of admitting defeat, I leaned into the joke. With a grin, I insisted the machine wasn't calibrated properly, that it wasn't giving me the points I *should* have received. Every miss became a playful excuse, every bad throw a reason to laugh harder.

Ashira rolled her eyes, her confidence unshaken, while Chris egged me on, laughing at my ridiculous claims. The three of us were caught in that perfect rhythm of drinking games— competitive but carefree, teasing but affectionate. My cheeks flushed, my words slurred, but I didn't care. I was having fun, wrapped in the warmth of friendship, pretending I was winning even as the scoreboard told another story.

For a while, it was easy to forget everything else. Easy to forget Matthew sitting at the bar, watching. His eyes followed us, almost angrily, though that didn't make sense. Matthew doesn't get angry... right?

Later, as I walked toward the bathroom near where he was sitting, his voice cut through the noise. Loud, sharp, reckless.

"I'm single as fuck," he yelled to the bartender. Then, without hesitation, he asked for her number.

The words hit me like a slap. In that moment, the room

seemed to tilt. The laughter from the darts faded, the holiday cheer blurred. All I could hear was his voice, all I could feel was the sting of bad faith disguised as bravado.

I slipped into the bathroom, the walls closing in around me, my chest tight with the echo of his words. I leaned against the sink, trying to steady my breath, but the sting of betrayal kept replaying in my head.

A few minutes later, the door creaked open and Briana stepped inside. She was young, in her twenties, with dark brown hair that looked like it sometimes got washed, sometimes not— probably depending on how quickly she'd rolled out of bed that day. There was a casualness to her, a kind of unpolished honesty that made her presence feel real. She was Matthew's best friend's girlfriend, but in that moment she wasn't there for him—she was there for me. She had heard what he said, seen the way I crumbled, and her eyes carried a kind of sincerity I hadn't expected.

"Hey," she said softly, her voice low and steady. "I saw what happened. You don't deserve that."

I shook my head, unable to form words, but she stayed close, grounding me with her presence.

"Breathe," she whispered, touching my arm lightly. "You're okay. He's being an idiot, but you're okay. Don't let his noise drown you out."

Her words cut through the panic, gentle but firm, and slowly the tightness in my chest began to ease. She stayed with me until my breathing steadied, until I could look at myself in the mirror without flinching.

When I finally walked out, I went straight to Matthew. My car was still at work—he had insisted on driving me and bringing me back—and I was too drunk to argue. So I told him to take me home. The night had already broken something in me, and all I wanted was to leave.

When I told him I wanted to leave, he brushed it off with a casual, "Let's go to Bar Louie." I said fine, but we had to stop by his car first. The moment we pulled up, the dizziness hit me hard. I opened the back door, leaned out, and started vomiting—first all over his back seat, then onto the pavement outside.

Briana came over quickly, patting my back, whispering that it would be over soon. Her voice was steady, almost maternal, and for a moment I believed her. Matthew, on the other hand, slammed the door shut on me while I was still heaving, locking me inside like I was cargo. Ten minutes later, he slid into the driver's seat and started the car, heading toward what I thought was home.

I must have passed out, because the next thing I remember was the sound of his phone ringing. It was his cousin. Matthew laughed into the receiver, saying he had "Shawty" with him. His cousin asked which one, and Matthew replied, "Shawty shawty," like I was nothing more than a punchline. He told him to come by, to bring food, because the party wasn't over yet—even though I was slumped in the back, drunk and barely conscious.

I opened my eyes just enough to see the highway sign: *Fall River, next exit.* Panic surged through me. I yelled at him to take me home, that I didn't want to go with him. His response was rage—screaming at me for ruining the night, rolling all the windows down so the freezing air tore through the car. My stomach twisted, the sickness worse than before. I threatened to open the back door if he didn't let me out. That's when he snapped, turned his head, and said, "Shut the fuck up, you stupid bitch," before taking the next exit then swinging the car around toward my home.

Then Briana called. Her voice was different now, stripped of the sincerity she'd shown in the bathroom. She told him how bad she felt for him, how hard it must be to deal with me. As if I was the problem. As if she hadn't just seen me break down, hadn't just comforted me minutes earlier. I sat there stunned, wondering why she was calling him at all. Wasn't she his best friend's girlfriend? Why was she suddenly siding with him, erasing what he had done, making me the villain in a story I hadn't written?

It reminded me of a time early on, when Matthew and I had just started dating. We were at a corporate cookout, and Briana and I slipped into the bathroom together, taking shots and laughing until the room spun. Later that night, as I drove her back to the office to pick up her car, the mood shifted.

We started talking about Matthew, about the little things he did that felt sweet to me. I told her how he had slipped an *I love you* into a conversation not long before, and how it had caught me off guard in the best way. But instead of smiling with me, Briana broke down. She cried hysterically, saying he always threw the word *love* around, that it meant nothing to him. Through her tears she warned me: he does whatever he wants, he'll never be good for me, and I needed to know that—because I'm a sweet girl, and she didn't want to see me hurt.

She cried as if she carried the pain of a thousand girls he might have dated before me. As if she was one of them. I found myself calming her down, even though her grief felt heavier than mine.

And then Matthew started calling. His name lit up my phone, his voice sweet and playful when I answered, asking where I was. I told him I was already at work, waiting for him to tell me the next move.

The second I hung up, Briana leaned in, eyes still glassy, and whispered that I had to pinky promise not to tell him anything she'd just said. Like she needed that promise more than she needed to breathe.

At the time, I brushed it off, convinced her tears were misplaced. But looking back, I see it differently. That night wasn't just drunken drama—it was a warning. Her words were the first cracks in the illusion I had built around Matthew, cracks I refused to see until they split wide open later.

So there I was, trapped in the backseat of his car, shivering in the freezing cold. He had forced me inside, and eventually we pulled up to my place. The moment the car stopped, I stumbled out, desperate to get inside, but he followed close behind.

I turned on him, my voice sharp and broken. I told him I had heard everything. I called him mean, a liar. I called him out for the bartender he had asked to exchange numbers with. None of it stopped him. He followed me into the house anyway.

I cried, I vomited again, and I begged him to leave. But he wouldn't. He just stood there in my kitchen, silent, watching me unravel—as if his eyes were saying, *Are you done yet?*

Finally, exhausted, I quieted and asked why he was still there. I told him to go to his cousin. He shook his head. "No," he said, "I love you. I'm sorry. I didn't mean it." Then he grabbed me, pulled me closer. I knew he could smell the sickness on me, taste the throw-up still clinging to my breath, yet he kissed me anyway. He promised he'd do better, that he hadn't known what he was doing.

And in my drunken state, I let him stay. I showered, we had sex, I vomited again, and then I passed out. As I laid my head against his chest, I told myself he didn't mean it. That he really was going to change for me. That he just didn't know what real love was—maybe no one had ever shown him.

But beneath that fragile hope was a voice I tried to silence. It whispered that I already knew better. That his apologies were just words, the same words Briana had warned me about. Still, I clung to the fantasy that my love could teach him, that my passion could fix what was broken. Even as the cracks widened, I convinced myself they were only shadows, not signs of collapse.

The next morning, he woke up early, made me breakfast, and stayed in bed with me all day while we recovered from the alcohol and the chaos of the night before. I didn't tell anyone what had happened—I couldn't. For a while, I carried it alone, convincing myself he wanted to change. I told myself I could feel his soul begging to be saved.

But after that night, things with Briana were never the same. Whenever she saw us together, she'd give me looks—sharp, disappointed—as if Matthew's choice to stay with me was beneath her.

Meanwhile, life at work demanded everything from me. I was excelling, but it came at a cost. Most nights I stayed up late, logged into the electronic systems, rewriting procedures line by line. The company had announced it would be splitting within the next year, and I was tasked with preparing all the documents for the transition. It was meticulous work— balancing global standards with the freedom to define our own processes, making sure every draft could reference global documents now but be easily untangled later when we stood alone.

I lived inside those systems, clicking through endless screens, revising workflows, building templates that would outlast the split. Every update had to be precise, every change tracked, every procedure aligned with compliance yet flexible enough to evolve. It was exhausting, but it was also proof to myself that I was capable, that I could carry the company through change. And in those long nights, when my eyes burned from staring at the screen, Matthew's presence at home felt like relief. He was the warmth waiting for me when I shut the laptop, the reminder that I wasn't alone.

That whole end of the year, he was kind. He cooked dinner for me and the kids, showed up at my son's basketball games when my ex didn't, asked questions about their hobbies, and listened. On Christmas Eve, he even dressed as Santa, delivering presents with a smile that lit up the room.

I introduced him to my mother, proudly calling him my boyfriend. For months, things felt good—better than good. We weren't drinking as much, we were laughing more, finding joy in simple things. We'd take walks together, meeting at different trails and claiming them as ours. We'd take the kids "ice skating," which was really just us sliding around in boots on a frozen pond hidden deep in the woods. Alfonzo would collect special sticks, declaring himself the master of the walks, the boss of the woods, telling us when to stop and when to go.

We all had fun. We were building something that looked like a solid connection. My son grew attached to him quickly, and I let myself believe that maybe, just maybe, Matthew was becoming the man I had hoped he could be.

Still, beneath the laughter and the dinners, there was vulnerability. Letting him into our lives meant opening doors I had kept locked for years. It meant trusting him with my children's hearts, with the fragile rhythm of our family. That was the risk—the fear that if he broke me, he would break them too.

But the way he showed up, the way he filled the empty spaces, made it feel worth the risk.

It was as if he was the missing piece we hadn't known we needed. With him, the house felt fuller, warmer. My children's laughter carried differently when he was around, echoing through the rooms like we were finally whole. And I let myself believe in that wholeness, even as the memory of his rage lingered in the shadows.

But at work, little things chipped away at that belief. One time, as we walked down the hall together, Mary—someone he had once messed around with—called Matthew's name in a way that made my skin crawl. It wasn't casual; it was drawn out, almost moaned, dripping with familiarity. She was Hispanic, around forty-five but looked ten years younger, with her surgically perfected curves—fake breasts, fake ass, the kind of body that demanded attention. The way she said his name made me feel like there was still something between them, some bond I wasn't aware of.

Shortly after that moaning of his name, I stopped her in the hall. My voice was calm, but deliberate. "Aren't you happily married?" I asked.

She blinked stupidly, then replied quickly, "Yes... why?"

I held her gaze. "Didn't seem like you were too happy, that's all."

Her face tightened, and instead of brushing it off, she followed me down the hall, trailing behind me until we reached my area—where Matthew was already waiting, holding snacks like he had planned to surprise me. The timing made everything sharper, more uncomfortable. She turned to him immediately, her voice edged with suspicion.

"Why she asking me this? What you saying to her?"

Her tone was accusatory, as if I had no right to question her, as if Matthew had stirred something between us.

I stood my ground. My voice was steady, even though my heart raced. "I just wanted to make sure we have a clear understanding," I said. "I'm happy too—with my boyfriend—and I'd like to keep it that way."

The words hung in the air, heavy and deliberate. I wasn't asking for permission, I was setting boundaries. I wanted her to know that whatever history she and Matthew had, whatever familiarity lingered in the way she said his name, it had no place in the life I was building.

Matthew stood there silently, snacks still in his hands, caught between us. And in that moment, I understood—this wasn't just about her. It was about me claiming my place, refusing to let the shadows of his past dictate the future I was trying to build.

Because we all worked together, I knew I couldn't confront her openly. I had to move in silence, to send my final message without exposing myself. So I chose creativity over confrontation. Through ShipADick, I sent Mary exactly what she deserved—a bag of dicks and one giant one, delivered anonymously, with the clear intention that she leave my Asian, my Coffee, my Matthew alone.

It was crude. It was bold. But it was mine—a silent strike, a way of reclaiming my voice in a situation where she had tried to erase it. And that bag of dicks? A mouthful for her, I'm sure—one that would keep her busy explaining herself to her husband, and ultimately keep things quiet for me and Matthew. Sometimes the loudest message isn't shouted in a crowded room; it's delivered quietly, dripping with sarcasm and defiance, impossible to ignore.

That day, a bag of dicks spoke louder than I ever could.

14

Book Club

Matthew wasn't living with me, but two days out of the week he was completely mine. Those nights felt sacred, like proof that he wanted us, that he was still choosing me. He showed up with dinners, with laughter, with promises. And yet, even in those moments, there were situations I couldn't ignore.

He hated my neighbor. Always tried to talk down about him, about my relationship with him. He accused me of sleeping with him, even though every time I went over there, Matthew was invited. The door was unlocked, and he could come whenever he wanted. There was nothing hidden, nothing secret. Still, he carried suspicion like a weapon, ready to use it against me.

One night, I thought he was coming earlier than midnight, maybe right after work. But he was a no-show. I assumed he must have been busy with homework, maybe forgot to tell me. So I texted him, asked what he was up to.

"Laundry, making dinner," he replied.

I asked if he was still coming over. He said yes, he'd be by before ten. That struck me as odd. How much laundry could one person have, especially when he had just done it a few days ago? And homework—hours of it? Really? Something about it didn't sit right, but I let it go. I told him I'd be at the neighbor's to kill time.

His reply came back: *"Bet."*

To us, "bet" was a word loaded with meaning. On the surface it meant *cool,* but underneath it carried the sting of *fuck you.* It was dismissive, sharp, a way of shutting me down without saying it outright. And "bet" wasn't the only trigger word between us. We had others—rules we made, codes we lived by. For instance, if I ever talked about me and Matthew, it had to be referred to as *us. US* couldn't say *we,* because *we* was dead. Even our inside jokes became trigger words, little reminders of the fragile line we walked. Every conversation where *we* would have been the proper word had to be replaced with *us,* because in our minds, *we* no longer existed.

Honestly, the name Zhi had something to do with it too. I told Matthew about him. Zhi reminded us of the word *we,* and Zhi sucked so the word itself felt poisoned. So *us* became the correct terminology.

I told him I was reading a book with my neighbor, one we were reading at work in book club. He didn't say much else, just another *"bet."* But I could feel the anger simmering through the silence.

A couple of hours passed, and then I heard footsteps on the stairs outside the neighbor's home. Matthew. He let himself in, beers in hand.

I was sitting across the kitchen table from my neighbor, the book open between us, pages spread like evidence of my transparency.

Before Matthew even sat down, I could feel the anger boiling under his skin. His presence filled the room with tension, heavy and suffocating. I didn't understand why. I had been honest. I had told him where I was, what I was doing. He had said he was busy. And it was only eight o'clock—earlier than he had promised.

The way he looked at me wasn't just anger—it was accusation. His eyes darted between me and my neighbor, as if searching for proof of something that wasn't there. My stomach twisted, not because I had done anything wrong, but because I knew nothing I said would convince him otherwise.

I tried to stay calm, to remind myself that I had been transparent. But the silence between us was louder than any words. My neighbor shifted uncomfortably, sensing the storm brewing, while Matthew cracked open a beer like it was armor.

In that moment, I realized how fragile the peace between us really was. Two days a week he was mine, but even then, suspicion followed us like a shadow. His kindness at home, his laughter with my kids, the dinners —all of it could be undone in an instant by the paranoia he carried.

And I sat there, across the table, wondering how long I could keep convincing myself that love alone would be enough to quiet the storm inside him.

The neighbor felt the tension too. It wasn't just me sitting there across the table, book open, trying to steady my breath. The air shifted the moment Matthew walked in, beers in hand, his jaw tight, his eyes scanning the room like he was searching for evidence.

My neighbor leaned back slightly, his posture stiff, the book still open in front of him. He didn't say anything, but I could see it in the way his eyes flickered between us—he knew this wasn't just a casual visit. He could feel the storm brewing under Matthew's skin, the anger that had walked in with him.

The words on the page blurred for me. I tried to focus, to keep reading, to prove that I was exactly where I said I'd be, doing exactly what I said I was doing. But Matthew's silence was louder than anything. My neighbor cleared his throat, a small sound that seemed to echo in the room, as if he was trying to break the tension without stepping into it.

I wanted to scream that there was nothing to hide, that I had been transparent, that Matthew had no reason to doubt me. But instead, I sat there, my neighbor across from me, both of us caught in the weight of Matthew's suspicion.

It was a strange kind of triangle—me, Matthew, and the neighbor—each of us aware of the unspoken accusations hanging in the air. My neighbor's eyes softened, almost sympathetic, as if he understood the position I was in. He didn't need to say it; his silence told me he felt the pressure too.

And in that moment, I realized it wasn't just me who lived under the shadow of Matthew's paranoia. Anyone near me could feel it, could sense the way his anger seeped into the room, changing the air, changing the way we moved, the way we spoke, the way we breathed.

It was like I belonged to him, not as a girlfriend, not as a woman he loved, but as something he owned. His eyes, his silence, the way he walked into a room and filled it with suspicion — it all carried the same message: *you are mine, and no one else has permission to touch you, speak to you, or share space with you.*

Every interaction I had outside of him seemed to trigger that possessiveness. My neighbor, my coworkers, even casual conversations — he treated them as threats, as if they were trespassing on territory that was marked by him. It wasn't about trust, it wasn't about love. It was about control.

The night at my neighbor's, when Matthew walked in with beers and anger simmering under his skin, I felt it more than ever. I wasn't just a woman sitting at a table reading a book—I was his property, at least in his mind. My presence there was already a betrayal. He didn't need proof. The fact that I was with someone else, even in innocence, was enough to ignite his rage.

Matthew sat down next to me, sliding into the chair where my feet had been resting. Out of habit, I tried to put my foot back on the edge of his chair, the way it had been before he sat down. He pushed it off without a word, a small gesture that carried more weight than it should have. It was a reminder: *this space is mine now, not yours.*

Trying to cut the tension, my neighbor offered Matthew some coffee. Matthew didn't miss a beat—"I heard you have the best coffee in town," he said, his tone sharp, more provocation than compliment. Then his eyes landed on the mug next to me, the one that read *my favorite neighbor got me this mug.* "Where'd you get that mug?" he asked him, knowing damn well it was a gift meant for me.

My neighbor kept it light, answering, "Oh, nowhere fancy, some corner store selling them." But Matthew didn't want the coffee. He didn't want the mug. He wanted to stir trouble, to remind me and everyone in the room that his presence carried weight, that even the smallest things could be twisted into a challenge.

I tried to ignore it, tried to keep my focus on the book in front of me. The story was about a man accused of possessing a gun he had purchased, even though he was a convicted felon. The jury was deciding whether he was guilty—because technically, the store had allowed him to buy it, and technically, when the police stopped him, the gun wasn't in his possession at all. Only a receipt suggested he had bought one. It was complicated, layered in technicalities, and I wanted to lose myself in the words, to escape the tension simmering beside me.

But Matthew wouldn't let me.

He started talking about guns. At first casually, but then sharper, more pointed. He asked my neighbor if he had any in the house. Then he asked if he knew how to use one. He kept circling back to it—guns, and the neighbor—like he was testing him, like he was pushing for something beneath the surface.

It was almost like a threat. No, it *felt* like a threat. The way his voice carried, the way his eyes lingered, the way he wouldn't let the subject go. My stomach twisted, my pulse quickened. This wasn't conversation. This was intimidation.

I looked at my neighbor, my best friend, the man who had always been there for me and my kids. His face had changed. His eyes flicked toward me, and I could see the question written there: *How are you with this guy? How is this man threatening me in my own home?*

The shame hit me hard. I felt so bad, so guilty, dragging this storm into the one place where I had always felt safe. My neighbor didn't deserve this. He had been nothing but supportive, nothing but kind. And yet here we were, sitting at his kitchen table, with Matthew turning the air into something sharp and dangerous.

I couldn't take it anymore. I told my neighbor I wanted to call it a night. My voice was steady, but inside I was unraveling. I could see the disappointment in his eyes, the disbelief, the silent judgment. And all I could do was gather myself, stand up, and decide it was time to go home—knowing walking out the door would mean Coffees with me, because that was the choice

I had made.

After we left my neighbor's place, Matthew and I got home and the tension boiled over. What started as sharp remarks turned into a full-blown argument. His voice rose, mine cracked, and every word felt like a strike. He accused, I defended, but nothing landed right. Finally, he snapped, his anger spilling out in the cruelest way: *"Just go to the neighbor's, go fuck him then."*

The words hit like a slap, cutting deeper than anything else he'd said. It wasn't just an insult—it was dismissal, rejection, a way of pushing me out while twisting the knife. And then he left, storming out and slamming the door, leaving me alone in the wreckage of his rage.

The next morning, before I left for work, my neighbor approached me. His face was serious, his tone steady. He told me that going forward, my kids were still welcome to play with his son, but he couldn't take any risks. He had to protect his home, his child. He said he didn't want to ever feel threatened in his own space again. He asked me to collect the things I had left at his place and, essentially, to leave him alone.

I broke down crying. I couldn't even bring myself to tell neighbor that I had kicked Matthew out the night before. In that moment, I felt distraught, broken. My neighbor—my AAA, my book nerd, the cock-rock collector of quirks and laughter— suddenly hated me. And all I could do was cry.

But when he saw me crying, something shifted. He came back over, his expression softer now, regret flickering in his eyes. He apologized for how he had spoken to me, said he hadn't meant to upset me, only that he needed to feel safe. He admitted he felt bad, that he didn't want me to hurt. He wanted me to cheer up.

His compassion in that moment cut through the heaviness. It was such a stark contrast to Matthew's rage the night before. Where Matthew had clenched his fists and spit fire, my neighbor opened his hands and offered understanding. Where Matthew had accused and threatened, my neighbor reassured and explained.

I told him the truth—that I had kicked Matthew out, and that I wasn't even sure if Matthew and I were together anymore. Saying it out loud felt like peeling back a layer of denial. I was grieving the loss of Matthew, even if I didn't want to admit it. My neighbor seemed to know, and he tried to help me forget the pain with jokes, brushing it off with a casual, "It's just a bitches cold, it'll all resolve itself," as if heartbreak were something you could sleep off.

One afternoon, I showed him a birthmark I had, and he laughed, "Whoa, that a gunshot wound?" To keep the mood light, we spun a whole story out of it—how no man, probably nothing on this earth, could have hurt me as badly as the time I got shot. We even joked about how I used to be right-handed but after the "gunshot" I had to start all over with my left. For a moment, the laughter eased the ache.

My neighbor would listen, nod, and though he didn't have real answers for me, his presence reminded me what respect and care looked like.

It took two weeks of ignoring Matthew's lame apologies before I even considered letting him back in. The texts, the calls, the half-hearted "I'm sorry" messages all felt empty, like words strung together without accountability. I thought I was done with him. I kept telling myself I was still going through a divorce, that my kids and I deserved better—someone stable, someone ready for commitment, someone who wouldn't accuse me based on his own past wrongdoings.

But Matthew didn't stop. And then his friend Tai started showing up at my job. Tai would corner me in the hallway or stop by my desk, telling me how much Matthew really wanted me back, how he was miserable without me, how he couldn't stop talking about me. Tai would go on and on—"He loves you, he knows he messed up, he wants to fix it, he wants to be better."

I listened, but inside I rolled my eyes. It was blabla, noise, another attempt to wear me down. If Matthew wanted me back, he needed to show me himself, not send his friend to campaign for him. Still, Tai's persistence chipped away at the wall I had built. It reminded me that Matthew wasn't letting go, that he was desperate enough to involve someone else.

Two weeks later, I got home from work and saw the kids outside, playing through our yards. Even though my relationship with the neighbor was fractured, we still spoke occasionally. He was kind enough to keep the kids' friendship intact, even if ours couldn't be the same. He respected me and the kids enough not to shut them out.

That's when I saw it—a silver car pulling into the neighbor's driveway. Matthew.

Instead of going inside, I slipped into my own car. I wanted to watch, to make sure my neighbor was okay. I needed to know why Matthew was there. From across the way, I saw him carrying books, a new heat-activated Rubik's cube, his movements stiff with nervousness. He knocked on the neighbor's door.

My neighbor opened it, his body language cautious, like he was ready to tell Matthew to go away—but in his usual gentle tone, because that's just the way he is. Matthew must have insisted, must have begged for just a moment, because soon I saw them both outside together. From where I sat, it looked like Matthew was crying, though I was too far away to be sure.

Moments later, Matthew walked back to his car. He didn't come toward me. He was leaving. I felt a rush of panic, honked my horn hard to get his attention. His brake lights flared, and then he turned left, circling back toward me.

I quickly called my neighbor. He told me Matthew had apologized, but asked if we could talk later. He didn't want to influence whatever conversation Matthew and I were about to have.

Matthew pulled back up, and this time I could see it clearly—he was crying. His face was red, his voice cracked. He told me he was wrong, that I had been right all along. He admitted he should never have accused me. He said he finally understood that my neighbor was my closest friend, a huge help with my kids, and that he had disrespected something sacred.

He apologized again and again, desperate. He said he loved me, loved my kids, that he wanted us to work. He didn't want to let us go. He wanted to prove his commitment.

To me, proving it meant more than words. It meant him seeing me more, staying with us, growing with me and my children. It meant commitment, stability, the thing I had been craving all along. And in that moment, with his tears and his desperation laid bare, I let myself believe he meant it.

When Matthew said he truly wanted us to work, I let myself believe him. I wanted to believe him. After weeks of lame apologies, after Tai showing up at my job trying to convince me he was serious, after the tears and the desperation in the neighbor's driveway—it felt different this time.

It felt, for the first time, like he finally understood what was at stake. The love I carried for him was unmatched, the connection between us undeniable, raw, and real. At home, the rhythm began to shift. He started coming around more often, staying longer, weaving himself into the fabric of our daily lives.

The kids noticed immediately. Their faces lit up when he walked through the door, their laughter louder, their energy brighter. My son would wake up in the mornings and the first thing he did was look for Matthew, making sure he was there to say good morning. My daughter searched for him too, but in her own way—she looked for him when she wanted humor, when she needed someone to tease her, to make her laugh. The rides to dance became their stage, filled with playful banter back and forth, something I knew she had never had with her own father.

And for me, it wasn't just the daytime rhythm—it was the late nights that made it feel real. The quiet hours when the kids were asleep and it was just us, talking about our past lives, the families we came from, the trauma within us. We opened wounds and shared scars, sometimes with tears, sometimes with laughter, sometimes with silence that said more than words ever could.

We watched movies together, curled up on the couch, sometimes serious, sometimes silly. Family Guy nights became our ritual, the kind of laughter that shook the walls and reminded me how good it felt to be light again. And in between those shows, there was the sex—wild, consuming, and unlike anything I had ever experienced before. Matthew wasn't just the best sex of my life; he was the only one who made it feel like more than sex, like it was *us*. It was love fucking, raw and unfiltered, the kind that made time disappear. His hands on me weren't just touches—they were claims, explorations, worship. Every kiss carried heat, every thrust carried urgency, and every moment felt like we were burning the world down just to exist together.

When I rode him, I would cum so hard it felt like my body was breaking open into color, like we were fucking until we saw rainbows. The release was overwhelming—waves of pleasure that left me shaking, gasping, laughing, sometimes even crying from how much it consumed me. We would go for hours, stopping only long enough to catch our breath, slick with sweat, the sheets twisted beneath us, the sound of our bodies filling the silence between episodes. Then we'd start again, because the hunger never really stopped.

It wasn't just sex—it was *us.* The rhythm, the passion, the way we fit together felt like something no other human on earth could replicate. In those nights, between laughter and exhaustion, between Family Guy jokes and whispered confessions, I wasn't broken, I wasn't exhausted—I was alive, wanted, whole.

The kids didn't see the cracks, the fire, the suspicion that haunted me. They saw only the man who cooked dinner, who played games, who made them feel like we were whole—like we were a family again. And in those late nights, in the laughter, the conversations, and the passion, I saw it too.

I wanted that stability, that commitment, the promise that he wouldn't drift in and out of our lives like a shadow. For a while, it felt like healing, as if the chaos had finally loosened its grip.

But beneath the surface, I carried both hope and fear. Hope that his words were more than just another phrase meant to keep me tethered. Fear that the fire I had seen before—the clenched fists, the accusations, the threats—wasn't gone, only waiting for its chance to return.

Still, I leaned into hope. I opened my home, my trust, and my children's laughter to him. I gave him space to grow with us, to prove he could become the man he claimed he wanted to be. I let myself believe that maybe—just maybe—this time would be different. Because what we had felt real, and I wanted to believe it could last.

But hope has a way of blinding us, and the path ahead would show me how easily belief can shatter.

15

The Verdict and the Promise

I thought the chaos was finally settling. Matthew and I were finding our rhythm, the kids were laughing again, and for a moment it felt like we were building something real. But for a while, we pushed our problems to the side. The arguments, the suspicion, the fire that had burned between us—they were still there, but they had to wait. We told ourselves we would deal with them later, maybe in couples therapy, maybe when life wasn't so heavy. Right then, there was something bigger demanding my attention.

Because once Miguel found out about Matthew and me, everything shifted. The man who had barely been present for the past year, who had spoken in little more than silence since his absence, suddenly wanted to play the role of father again. Not out of love, not out of responsibility, but out of spite. The moment he knew Matthew and I were official, he came crashing back into our lives, determined to make me pay.

He threatened Matthew one day while picking up the kids, telling him to get out of *his* house—the house he had abandoned, the home he had left behind. I couldn't believe it. The man of few words, the man who had vanished from their lives, now wanted to storm back in, pretend he had always wanted to be around them, and threaten to take them from me. He told me he would fight for custody, that he would have the kids taken away.

During the kids' April vacation, he asked if he could take them for the week. I was working, so honestly it helped. It would have been a relief—anyway, that's what I thought. But not even twenty-four hours later, he called me screaming to pick up our daughter. She had gotten her period and told him she needed to shower, needed clean clothes. He wanted her to put her dirty clothes back on and go to dance. When she refused, he lost control. He called me, screaming, demanding I pick her up. The way he was acting—erratic, unstable—I told him I would, but only if I could pick up both kids. He agreed, until I showed up.

Ella came into the car and told me there was no food in the house. Leftovers from the day before had been stretched into lunch and dinner. No milk, no water. They had to ask the neighbor for food, snacks, or drinks if they needed anything. Miguel had already called the police, telling them he wanted to make sure I was only taking Ella. When I arrived, I showed the officers the messages. My daughter told them what had happened. The cop stopped us mid-sentence and said, "Everything you're saying would mean DCF would get involved." I looked him in the eye and said, "Maybe they should be then because its wrong." He stared back, cold, and said, "Listen, you don't want DCF involved. Your son is okay with staying. Just let him stay since there's no order in place."

I couldn't believe it. I remained calm, asked to give Alfonzo a hug goodbye, and drove away in disbelief. Even then, I didn't go after him for custody. Not when he kept Alfonzo four days longer than he said he would. Not when he broke his word again and again. No. It wasn't until the kids were in camp that summer that I finally filed for sole custody.

When the summer months came I signed the kids up for camp. It was a random Tuesday when Miguel randomly called and threatened to take the kids from camp that he could do what he wanted and not return them. That was the day everything changed. His words weren't just empty threats anymore—they carried the kind of danger I couldn't ignore. I left work early, my heart pounding, my mind racing through every possible outcome. Matthew left early with me, standing by my side as if to remind me I wasn't alone in this fight.

We walked into the courthouse together, the air heavy with the kind of silence that only comes when you know your life is about to shift. I could feel the weight of every step, the echo of my heels against the floor like a drumbeat pushing me forward. My hands shook as I filled out the paperwork, but my resolve was steady. This wasn't about me anymore. It was about protecting my children, about making sure they were safe from the chaos Miguel had dragged back into our lives.

I filed for emergency sole custody that day. The words themselves felt unreal, like they belonged to someone else's story, but they were mine. They were my children's. And as I signed my name, I knew I had crossed a line I could never uncross. Miguel had forced my hand, and now the fight was official. I was granted temporary sole custody.

Matthew squeezed my hand as we walked out of the courthouse. For a moment, I let myself breathe. For a moment, I believed that maybe this was the beginning of something stronger—something that would finally give my kids the stability they deserved.

Temporary sole custody only lasted ten days before we were both ordered back to court for a battle I knew all too well. What hurt me most was that it had come to this—that Miguel wasn't willing to simply be there for the kids without letting his ego, wounded because I had moved on, drive everything. He didn't have to threaten me, but he did. And I loved my children too much to risk losing them during one of his angry episodes.

When I arrived at the family probate courthouse, I didn't know what to expect. I had spent the entire week before gathering evidence—documented threats, proof of his poor choices, the constant hostility that had flared up only because I was dating someone new. Matthew and my mom walked in with me. Miguel showed up twenty minutes late, with a lawyer at his side.

They sent us all downstairs into an old brick building. The walls echoed with other families' battles. I could hear a mother cursing at a father in mediation, accusing him of beating their son, while he insisted it had been an accident years ago and demanded more rights. The pettiness between them was sharp, and I thought to myself, *I know what not to do.*

I sat between my mom and Matthew, waiting. Miguel's lawyer walked past me, sneered, "You're still married," then turned to Miguel and muttered, "Disgusting." They both laughed as if the whole thing were a joke.

Eventually, the mediator called us in. Only Miguel, his lawyer, and I were allowed in the room. They began by claiming I had kept the kids away, insisting there was no reason Miguel shouldn't have fifty-fifty custody. When it was my turn, I wanted to hand over the evidence I had collected, but the mediator didn't even want to look at it. Instead, he asked me to explain in my own words why we were there.

I stuck to what I had said when I filed, recounting the situations that had unfolded over the past year. I told him about the time Miguel tried to force Ella to put on dirty period underwear. As I spoke, Miguel interrupted, blurting out, "It was a few drops of blood—stop making this bigger than it was." Right there, he admitted to what I had put on paper.

I pointed out more: how he had threatened to kill himself when he stopped by to see the kids once. I had ten children running between my house and my neighbor's that day. Miguel pulled into my driveway, a wreck, and I went outside. He said it wasn't a good time for him to see the kids, then started yelling that he wanted to die, that he was going to kill himself. My children weren't standing there, but others were close enough to hear every word. I told him he needed to calm down and see a therapist.

Miguel turned to the mediator again, speaking out of turn, and said, "What would you do if you found out your wife was seeing someone else, that someone else was raising your kids?" The mediator looked at him and replied, "I would do whatever I had to do to be a good father and role model in their lives."

By the end, we couldn't reach an agreement. The mediator sent us to the judge.

When we entered the courtroom, Miguel sat behind me with his lawyer, talking loudly as if to fill the silence. He started bragging about how his dog had once fallen out of a window and how he had to think fast, perform emergency care, and save its life. He was lying. When that dog fell out the window, he had called me in a panic. Matthew was there too. Miguel had pulled up with the dog bleeding from a huge gash on its head, begging me to do something. We weren't even on good terms then, but I ran inside, grabbed antiseptic spray, bandages, and a powder I had bought years ago from Petco to stop bleeding when I clipped my own dog's nails too short. I wasn't even sure it would work. I told him to keep cleaning the wound, keep applying the powder, but that the dog probably needed a vet. He never took him. The dog lived, but not because of Miguel. Yet here he was, fabricating a story about how he had saved his dog—the dog I saved.

The judge listened, reviewed the mediator's notes, and then looked directly at me. "All Miguel wants is to have his kids with him. You're not allowing that," she said. Her words cut deep, not because they were true, but because they carried the authority of the bench. I stayed quiet, biting back the urge to defend myself right then, knowing it was all bullshit.

When it was my turn, I steadied my voice and said, "I know Miguel loves his children. But Miguel has undiagnosed mental health concerns that I truly feel need to be addressed before he's granted custody." I didn't raise my voice, I didn't let anger take over—I spoke plainly, because the truth was enough.

The judge paused, her expression unreadable, then said she would review the mediator's notes and that we would receive her decision in the mail. The words hung in the air, final yet unfinished, leaving me with the weight of uncertainty.

The waiting period was its own kind of trial. We did our best to keep routines normal, to keep life steady while the court's decision hung over us like a shadow. It was summertime, and the kids were still in camp. After camp, Matthew, the kids, and I would go for late afternoon bike rides.

Alfonzo hadn't known how to ride a bike before Matthew. One weekend, the three of us went to the Blackstone Valley bike path and dedicated ourselves to teaching him. From balancing on the grass to pushing him forward for a kickstart, Matthew and I stayed with him until he figured it out on his own. No training wheels, no shortcuts—just patience and encouragement. By the end of that weekend, Alfonzo was riding around like he had been doing it his whole life. Watching him transform from a boy full of doubts on the first day to a boy glowing with pride by the last was beautiful. We were all so proud.

After that, bike rides became our ritual. We rode through neighborhoods, up and down hills, weaving through trails and woods until it was time for dinner. But it wasn't just the rides— we filled our days with everything we could. We went to Great Wolf Lodge for the kids' birthdays, doubled-dipped at Six Flags more times than I can count, wandered through the Mystic Aquarium, spent afternoons at the library. You name it, we were doing it.

The Mystic Aquarium trip was supposed to be special. I had been thinking about it the whole week prior, excited to finally meet Matthew's brother, his brother's wife, and their son. But when the day came, the interaction felt like it lasted all of thirty seconds—barely enough time to say hello before it was over. It stung, but I told myself it was still better than nothing. The kids had fun, and we stayed longer, soaking in the tanks and exhibits, making the most of the day even if the family moment I had hoped for slipped away almost as soon as it arrived.

Matthew loved cooking, and he was good at it. Even when the kitchen felt like 110 degrees, he would come home, shower, cook, and then shower again from the heat. Every day we didn't take for granted. We took advantage of every minute we had together, all of us, while we waited for that verdict.

A month went by. Two weeks before school started, the envelope finally came. I felt it in my chest as I opened it, reading line by line. Miguel was granted two days in the summer with Alfonzo and two days consisting of three hours each with Ella. Once school started, he would only have Alfonzo one night a week on Sundays, and Ella for three hours every Sunday.

What the court didn't understand was how long it had taken to get Alfonzo to the happy place he was in. Alfonzo was happy. Ella was happy. And I knew they would be upset. I waited until after dinner to sit with them and talk individually.

Miguel treated Alfonzo differently. I think when I had him, Miguel put whatever effort he had into Alfonzo and stopped trying completely with Ella. The damage he had caused in those early years—his drinking, his outbursts—meant he could no longer manipulate her the way he could with Alfonzo. And now, even with the court's order, I could see the pain it brought them both.

Ella fought me on it until I showed her—it was court ordered. Alfonzo stayed quiet for a moment, then cried. He asked me if he could tell them he didn't want to go. Out of both kids, I thought Ella would be the one to resist, but I hadn't expected Alfonzo to be so broken by the decision.

I pulled them close and told them, "I will be right here waiting for you to come back. No matter what, you will always come back home." I encouraged Alfonzo, telling him, "Your daddy misses you, and I'm sure he'll try to do some fun things together."

I reminded the kids that no matter what the court said, no matter how many hours or days they had to spend away, they would always come back home. Home was where they were loved, where they were safe, where they belonged. I promised them I would be right here waiting every single time, and that nothing—not a judge, not Miguel, not anyone—could change that. I gave both of them strength with my words even when I felt my heart breaking, reminding them that they were loved, that they were capable of getting through this.

Alfonzo wiped his tears, Ella sat quietly, and I could see the strength beginning to settle in them. They didn't have to carry this alone. I would carry it with them.

And as I tucked them in that night, I whispered to myself as much as to them: *We will get through this. We will keep moving forward. And no matter how hard it gets, love will always bring us back home.*

16

Take Back Sunday

Sunday came faster than I wanted it to. I had cried all week in silence, never letting the kids see the weight I carried. Matthew saw. Matthew was basically living with us by then, even though he still had his own apartment. He hadn't left since June except to pick up more clothes. We were happy—truly happy. We went out as we always did, riding bikes, going on walks, just being together.

That morning, Alfonzo's bag was already packed. We thought it would be good for all of us to ride to Dunkin' Donuts before their dad arrived for the 10 a.m. court-ordered pickup. The ride took about twenty-five minutes, the summer air warm against our skin. Matthew and I shared a caramel swirl, Ella ordered a frappuccino, and Alfonzo sipped on a frozen hot chocolate.

We sat together at the table, laughing and making light jokes, trying to keep their headspace clear and happy before they had to go. One of our favorite running jokes was calling each other "Boss Baby." The kids always insisted Matthew was the real Boss Baby, while I was just "Boss Mommy." It became our way of teasing each other, a silly inside joke that kept things light even when the heaviness of the day pressed in.

We rode back with an hour to spare, and I had the kids shower and get dressed. The waiting was the hardest part. The first day, he showed up ten minutes late—as if the anticipation wasn't already unbearable, he made us wait longer. When he finally arrived, he told me they were having a birthday party for Alfonzo at his parents' house. One I hadn't been told about, one I wasn't invited to.

I gave them both big hugs and kisses before they left. Matthew, always playful, dabbed Alfonzo off like the buddies they had become. Ella flipped Coffees hat for a friendly goodbye. Watching them walk away, my heart clenched, but I held onto the hope that the strength we had built together—the bike rides, the laughter, the Boss Baby jokes—would carry them through the day.

Not long after the kids left that Sunday, Ella called me. She asked if she could stay with her dad longer. I was happy to hear it—figured she must have been having fun at the party, so I said yes. Matthew, always thoughtful, decided to plan a special day for us since we suddenly had more time. He wanted to keep my mind off the ache of not having the kids.

This was the first time I wouldn't have Alfonzo with me every day. He had only ever slept over at a friend's house twice in his whole life. I missed him too much, so I always encouraged the sleepovers at our house instead. Letting him go felt heavier than I expected. Matthew knew that, so he made reservations at a fancy restaurant in Newport, right by the ocean. Just the two of us.

We sat down, the waves crashing in the distance, the air salty and warm. Eleven minutes into our meal, my phone rang. It was Ella. Her voice was tight, urgent. She wanted us to pick her

159

up immediately.

I learned that my sister Alyssa had shown up. Ella didn't like Alyssa. Back during COVID, Alyssa had helped me by staying with the kids while I worked, since she worked from home. Ella hadn't been a fan even then, but that wasn't what ruined their relationship.

Alyssa wasn't a bad person, but she was a social worker—a social worker who needed to social work herself. She was dating Drew, a man our family already knew. He had once dated our cousin and had three beautiful daughters, my little cousins. But Drew was a terrible human being and a poor excuse for a father. He let his ex raise their kids, provided no support, and refused to take drug tests in court because he was on heroin.

There was a time when his middle daughter, Rain, was just two years old. Drew was supposed to be watching her while Anne, their mother, worked. He left his drugs out, nodded off playing video games, and Rain overdosed. She went into a two-day coma. Doctors scrambled to understand how a toddler could get hold of such a powerful drug. That was the day Anne left him.

But somehow Drew wormed his way into my sister's life, looking for support. Alyssa let him in, even gave him another child — a boy, his fourth chance to do right. But he didn't change. Before Alyssa ever dated him, Drew already had three daughters with our cousin Lynn. He wasn't a stranger to the family; he was the kind of man everyone wished would leave for good, the kind who drifted out just long enough for people to breathe, only to show up again attached to someone you love.

After the boy was born, Drew started sending nasty text messages to his daughters, blaming them for his absence. Long paragraphs, always with the same message: it was their fault, not his. Rain had been my cousin long before she became my favorite niece. She and Ella had also been close for years, long before Alyssa and Drew ever crossed paths. Rain told Ella everything — about the heroin, about finding needles in his arm when she was little, about the recent messages. I didn't like that my twelve-year-old was hearing all of this, but they were cousins, and it was all true. Ella asked me to talk to Alyssa, so I did.

I tried to warn my sister. I told her what Drew had been doing, that it was clear he was still on drugs. She flipped out, accused me of taking the girls' side over hers. It wasn't about sides—it was about right and wrong. As an adult, Drew should never have sent those messages. I even explained that Ella had asked me to talk to her. But Alyssa only got louder, yelling, "How could you do this to me?" before hanging up. That was what destroyed their relationship.

So when Ella called me from Miguel's house, saying she felt uncomfortable with Alyssa there, I believed her. She texted me in the middle of it all, saying Alyssa had started video recording her, snapping random photos. I told Miguel what Ella said, asked him to support her and tell Alyssa to stop. Instead, he turned on Ella, calling her selfish for wanting to go home. I heard his mother in the background blaming Ella too, saying she ruined everything and shouldn't have stayed.

Miguel told me I wasn't allowed to pick her up. But I knew the law. I had extended her stay under the condition that she was safe. She no longer felt safe, so Matthew and I left right away. One sip of our drink, food not even on the table yet—we walked out of that restaurant and drove to get her.

When we arrived at Miguel's parents' house, I already knew they would be looking for a reaction from me. Emergency pickups were never simple, and I understood how quickly things could escalate. To keep the peace, I asked Matthew to stay in the car so Miguel wouldn't have another excuse to get angry.

I walked around the huge porch, scanning their big backyard until I finally spotted Ella. On my way, Miguel's brothers tried to stop me, reaching out for hugs, but I shook my head and said, "Sorry, I'm just not okay with things right now. Maybe we can talk later." I kept walking.

I found Alfonzo and pulled him into one more big hug before leaving. Then I headed back toward the car with Ella. Matthew was vaping, and Miguel noticed as we walked. He immediately accused Matthew of doing drugs.

"It's a vape," I said firmly.

Miguel shot back, "Why is he vaping with my daughter about to be in the car?"

I kept my voice steady. "It's a Jeep with no doors or windows, and she's not in the car. I asked him to stay here to avoid causing issues."

Miguel kept making remarks, but I didn't stop. I kept walking to the car, climbed in, we all fastened our seat-belts quickly, and since it was already running, we pulled away.

Not long after, my phone lit up. Messages started pouring in — accusations that I was drunk, that I was on drugs, that something had to be "wrong" with me. Miguel, his brother, and his brother's wife all suddenly decided that the weight I'd lost could only mean one thing. Who says that?

Then there was Beth — his brother's wife — who had been a nurse for maybe three months and suddenly thought she was some kind of expert. She kept insisting, "based on her experience," that it *had* to be drugs. The irony wasn't lost on me. The last person who should've been commenting on anyone's body or health was her. And the comeback that flashed through my mind was sharp enough to cut: *If you wanted tips on losing weight, all you had to do was ask.*

But I didn't say it. I stayed quiet. Because I knew silence would burn them longer than anything I could've thrown back.

Instead, the next day I called my lawyer. She told me to document everything. So I went straight to my doctor and had a drug test done that same day. I kept the results, tucked them away for later, and said nothing. Sometimes silence is the only power you have left.

And that was how it went—the very first weekend in Miguel's care.

That following Tuesday, when Miguel showed up at my job screaming in the parking lot, I felt the chaos rising in my chest. His voice carried, his arms swung wildly, and for a moment it was just me standing there, exposed. But then Matthew arrived. He saw me outside, saw Miguel's aggression, and without hesitation came out to stand beside me.

Matthew didn't need to say much—his presence alone shifted the energy. Miguel had a pattern: he waited until Matthew wasn't around to harass me, to push me, to try to break me down. But when Matthew was there, Miguel backed off. He peeled out of the lot, tires screeching, because he knew when Matthew was around I was no longer someone he could intimidate.

With Matthew around, I felt safe in a way I hadn't in years. He didn't just protect me physically—though I knew he would step in if Miguel ever crossed that line—he protected me emotionally. He reminded me I wasn't alone in this fight. He gave me the strength to stand tall, to keep walking even when Miguel hurled accusations.

Matthew had this way of grounding me. His calmness, his

steady presence, his refusal to let Miguel's chaos seep into our lives—it all wrapped around me like armor. I knew Miguel wanted a reaction, wanted me rattled, but with Matthew there, I could breathe. I could hold my head high and walk back inside knowing I wasn't facing this battle by myself.

HR installed cameras after I reported what happened, and I thought, *Wow, they really care.* Even before the cameras, Matthew had already made me feel cared for. He was my shield, my anchor, the reason I could keep moving forward without letting Miguel's rage consume me.

I felt a strange mix of relief and weariness. Relief that someone cared enough to protect me, but weariness from living under constant attack. Matthew's presence gave me safety, yet the truth was, I was tired of always needing it. And sometimes, I couldn't shake the feeling that Matthew didn't mind Miguel stirring up trouble—that in those moments of chaos, he wanted to be seen stepping in, wanted his role as protector to be noticed.

Miguel craved disorder, and he got it. He wanted me rattled, and sometimes he succeeded. I went home that night drained— not triumphant, not broken—just tired. But even in that exhaustion, I knew I had to keep going. For Alfonzo. For Ella. For myself.

There was no victory, but there was resolve. I wasn't unshaken, but I was unbroken.

The rest of the workday slipped by faster than I expected. I ignored every call and text from Miguel, shutting him out completely. I was done engaging in his chaos, at least for now.

When the day finally ended, I picked up both kids from camp. Alfonzo ran into me with the world's biggest hug, squeezing me so tight I thought he'd never let go. That hug alone reminded me why I kept fighting through the exhaustion.

Back at home, Alfonzo discovered the surprise Matthew and I had prepared. His room and gaming area had been transformed—Matthew had carefully positioned each of his anime figures around the desk, blankets were fresh, the space spotless, everything waiting for him. Alfonzo's face lit up, and he kept thanking us over and over, his joy filling the house with a kind of light I hadn't felt in days.

In that moment, I remembered that even in the roughest times, I could still put my best foot forward. I had been depressed while they were gone, the silence pressing down on me. But I wanted Alfonzo's return to feel special, to show him how much he was loved and missed.

That night, surrounded by gratitude and laughter, I understood something simple but powerful: even if chaos pressed in from the outside, within these walls I could still build moments of peace, resilience, and love. Those moments became the reason I kept moving forward—because I knew the world beyond our door would keep testing us.

17

Backpacks and Broken Doors

School was starting soon, and the checklist of supplies seemed endless. The kids wanted everything just right, and I wanted them to feel prepared. We picked out their requested brand-new sneakers, the kind that squeak a little on polished floors until they're broken in.

Alfonzo settled on a red Nike bag—simple, sharp, and exactly his style. Ella, on the other hand, had her heart set on the Nike Elite bag. And of course, we got it... for the *modest* price of one hundred and twenty dollars. Because apparently, carrying notebooks and pencils requires a bag that costs almost as much as a car payment.

The aisles smelled of fresh paper and sharpened pencils. We stacked notebooks with crisp, untouched pages, each cover chosen carefully: one with anime characters, another with a sleek metallic finish. Packs of pens and highlighters in every color went into the cart, along with glue sticks, scissors, and rulers that seemed to promise order in the chaos of school days. Alfonzo insisted on mechanical pencils, while Ella wanted glitter gel pens that sparkled across the page.

Folders in every shade of the rainbow, binders with sturdy rings, sticky notes shaped like stars and hearts—all of it piled high until the cart looked like a celebration of possibility. Even lunchboxes were chosen with care, insulated and ready to carry their favorite snacks.

Miguel didn't offer a hand—not with the shopping, not with the expenses. Asking him for help was like pulling teeth, a draining effort that always ended in disappointment. So I stopped asking. Matthew stepped in instead, over and over. He covered the costs, from school supplies to hair appointments, quietly taking on the weight Miguel refused to carry.

He wanted to give me peace. And even in the silent chaos brewing between us, he kept playing his part—steady, present, determined to ease the burden where Miguel refused to. Surrounded by fresh shoes, new notebooks, and the sparkle of gel pens, I let myself breathe a little easier, knowing the kids would walk into school with everything they needed.

The morning of the first day of school came faster than I expected. My shift started at seven, so I couldn't be there for the send-off. It stung a little, missing that milestone, but Matthew filled the gap without hesitation.

He went in later—8:30—and made sure everything was handled. He packed their lunches, double-checking that each bag had the snacks they loved. He filled up their water bottles. On the way, he treated them to Dunkin' Donuts, a little ritual to sweeten the nerves of the first day. Then, with backpacks slung over their shoulders and smiles sticky with glaze, he lined them up for the traditional first day photos.

The pictures captured more than just fresh shoes and new notebooks—they caught the excitement, the nervous energy, the start of something new. And when the bus pulled up,

Matthew stood by, making sure they climbed aboard on time, waving until the doors closed.

Even though I wasn't there, I knew they were cared for. Matthew had stepped in, not just to cover what I couldn't, but to make sure the kids felt celebrated. In that moment, I realized that while chaos brewed in other corners of our lives, the kids still had stability, love, and a sense of normalcy to carry them into the school year.

For a while, everything seemed to fall into place. Life almost felt like a dream—steady, manageable, even hopeful. It wasn't until Storm, my cat, got out one night that things started to shift again between me and Matthew.

I had gone to bed early that Friday. Matthew was playing Fortnite with Alfonzo in his room, their laughter drifting faintly through the walls. I remember half-waking to the sound of whispers—someone calling out softly for Storm. Then the creak of a door opening. One of the kids. Matthew's voice followed, asking Alfonzo if he had seen her. I listened as he said, "We don't have to tell Mommy yet, let's just look first. She's sleeping."

At the time, I thought it was probably nothing. Storm was likely hiding, tucked away in one of her usual spots. I drifted back into sleep, not knowing how long I'd been out until Matthew came upstairs and asked if Storm might be in our bedroom. That jolted me awake. Storm wasn't just a pet—she was my other baby, fur or not. I loved her fiercely. She came right before the death of my dog Skitzo.

I grabbed my phone immediately and pulled up the cameras. If she had gotten out, I knew it would have been captured. As I scrolled through the footage, I saw Matthew back and forth outside and inside for nearly an hour, clearly searching.

My stomach sank. I couldn't believe I had fallen asleep the first time—I just hadn't thought she could have slipped out. Everyone knew the rule: doors closed, always.

Storm had only gotten out once before, when I took the trash outside. She had been waiting at the door, crying to come back in, terrified of the passing cars on the main road. That memory haunted me as I kept scanning the footage.

Then I saw it—five hours earlier. Matthew and Alfonzo had finished a bike ride and were heading inside. At the same time, groceries were being delivered. Alfonzo went in first, assuming Matthew was right behind him. But Matthew stopped when the delivery driver pulled up. He must have forgotten the door was wide open. Next thing I saw was him directing the driver to bring the groceries to the other front door.

The door had been left open for a long time. My cameras never even captured it closing—just Matthew moving in and out, searching, desperate. And somewhere in that gap, Storm had slipped away.

That first time Storm slipped out, I was frantic. I printed missing posters and taped them up around the neighborhood, desperate for any sign of her. Word spread quickly, and somehow Miguel found out. His response wasn't concern— it was venom. He told me I *deserved this*. Deserved to lose her, deserved the pain, all because of what I had "done to him" regarding our kids.

But all I had ever done was protect them from harm. That was my only crime in his eyes. Still, he twisted it, made me feel awful, degraded me in ways that cut deeper than I wanted to admit. Miguel always seemed to want to hurt me, to find the sharpest words and drive them in. And in that moment, when I was already broken searching for Storm, his cruelty nearly crushed me.

That night turned into a blur of desperation. We walked the streets for hours, calling out her name, our voices echoing into the dark. Flashlights cut through the night, treats rattled in bags, but nothing brought Storm back. The whole weekend became a vigil—I didn't leave the house, terrified that if she returned, I wouldn't be there to open the door.

I researched every method I could find for locating missing cats. I even fell for a scam—$350 for a supposed drone service that promised to track her down. I don't know how I believed it, but grief makes you reckless. Still, nothing worked. Nights of calling, crying, blaming Matthew, and Storm was nowhere.

One article warned against putting litter boxes outside, saying it might attract other animals. But I was willing to take that risk. In the middle of the night, Sunday into Monday, I carried her litter box outside. I went back in to grab her favorite canned food, planning to set it nearby. And then—just as I opened the door—Storm came running inside. Just like that, she was back. Relief washed over me in a flood.

But two weeks later, it happened again. Somehow Matthew left the door open, and Storm was gone. The pain was unbearable—too much, too soon. Between Miguel's chaos, the new school routines, and losing Storm twice in such a short time, I felt like I was breaking. I blamed Matthew. I yelled, told him I couldn't do this anymore, couldn't even look at him. How could he be so careless—again?

It was a Tuesday this time. I prayed for her return on Wednesday, my work-from-home day. I prayed in the woods, screaming to God to please bring her back. I wasn't giving up. I even slept in my car with the door open, hoping the litter box outside would draw her back. My heart was shut, but my hope was stubborn.

Wednesday came, and she was still gone. I prayed harder. Matthew searched too, but I couldn't accept that as an apology. She was still missing. I told him she'd be home by noon—I clung to that promise, made wishes, prayed again at 11:11.

On my lunch break, I had thirty minutes to search. I crossed the street into the woods, treats in hand, calling out, crying until my voice cracked. Twenty minutes passed, and I collapsed to my knees, defeated. Matthew was combing the streets, and I was alone in the woods, empty.

Then I heard it—the faintest meow. I turned, scanning the trees, and there she was. Storm lay under a tree, wounded. It looked like a hawk had attacked her—her head and eye injured, her body too scared or too weak to move. I scooped her up, screaming for Matthew. He heard me and rushed back, disbelief in his eyes when he saw her.

We had found her. Fragile, broken, but alive.

I finished my work-from-home shift as quickly as I could, and then we rushed to the vet. They examined her thoroughly— bones, cuts, the holes in her head, the damage to her eye. Miraculously, nothing was broken. She was lucky, they said. Terrified, but she could recover. They gave her medicine for the pain and sent us home.

Storm was back, fragile but alive. As I held her, I realized how much of myself I had poured into those nights of searching, praying, and refusing to give up. Miguel's cruelty, Matthew's carelessness, the endless chaos of school routines and daily battles—all of it had nearly broken me. But Storm's return reminded me that even in the darkest stretches, there can still be light.

She was terrified, wounded, but she was home. And in

her recovery, I saw my own. I had been battered by blame, exhaustion, and fear, yet I was still standing. Still fighting. Still protecting what mattered most.

The vet said she was lucky, but I knew luck wasn't the whole story. It was persistence, love, and the refusal to surrender. Storm's resilience became my reminder: no matter how many times the doors are left open, no matter how many storms circle around us, I will keep finding my way back.

18

Bruises and Broken Faith

At work, Briana was a different person whenever Matthew was around. She'd offer nothing more than a polite "hi," presenting herself as spotless, almost saintly. But I knew better. Behind that mask, her intentions were far from pure. It was frustrating, because I had helped her countless times — answering her questions, stepping in when she struggled, even taking on tasks she could have managed herself. I thought that kind of support meant we were friends, at least until the Christmas party. That night, she showed me just how easily kindness can be taken for granted, and revealed her true colors.

At work when he wasn't around, she made it her mission to tear me down. She'd walk past my office with cutting remarks, whispering that Matthew would leave me soon. She'd give me dirty looks, gossip to new employees I trained, and spread venom wherever she could. Yet in front of him, she acted innocent, as though none of it existed. And Matthew... he kept pretending not to acknowledge the damage she was trying to cause me no matter how many times I'd try to tell him.

But she didn't stop at petty comments. She escalated. She

even reached out to Jaison from QA Escalations, claiming there was a major discrepancy in their lab regarding a binder. Total nonsense — her boss and I had reviewed it the day before, and everything was perfectly fine. She went out of her way, more than once, to try to get me in trouble. Why? I don't know.

But when that "discrepancy" landed on his desk, Jaison messaged me immediately. He was tall and lean, with a calm, thoughtful look — the kind of guy who didn't say much, but when he did, it was either quietly brilliant or unexpectedly funny. He had this subtle humor that slipped out in one-liners, the kind that made you laugh harder because you never saw them coming. I told him straight up the claim was bullshit, and he laughed because he already knew. Between him and Briana's boss, they shut it down fast and made it clear she couldn't just escalate things for no reason. There was nothing wrong with the binder, nothing to fix, nothing to report.

Still, she never apologized. Not a word. Just more of the same petty, pointless nonsense.

And Jaison — he was the opposite of all that. Cool, steady, easy to be around. Matthew and I used to joke and call him "Hoison," like the sauce, and he never got offended. He'd just laugh, shake his head, and go back to whatever quiet genius thing he was doing.

My relationship with Matthew was already under strain. Custody battles with Miguel, the missing cat, the endless school routines, the house, the never-ending list of chores—it was all weighing Matthew down, and I could feel it pressing on me too. Briana's hostility only added another crack to the foundation, another reminder that even when things seemed steady, there were always forces working against me.

That weekend, with Miguel having the kids, Matthew and

I decided to treat ourselves. We wandered down the street and bought homemade pickles from the "pickle boy" nearby, savoring the simple joy of something fresh and local. Then we stumbled upon a church hosting an Egyptian festival.

We parked a few blocks away, and though there was an easier route to the church near where we left the car, something tugged at me to go the longer way. Matthew was annoyed, urging me to just walk through the closer entrance, but I told him there's always a reason. I didn't know what it was yet, but I trusted that pull.

We crossed to the other side of the street, heading toward the main road where the larger entrance stood. And that's when I saw him—a little boy, barely more than a toddler, in pajamas and diapers, wobbling on unsteady legs. He couldn't have been more than one or two years old. His walk was clumsy, the kind of gait that comes with just learning how to balance.

I froze, then turned to Matthew. "Are you seeing this?" I asked. The baby was alone. No parents, no siblings, no one nearby. He stumbled, nearly falling into the road, and my heart stopped. I rushed forward, scooping him up before he could tumble into traffic. "Okay," I whispered, "let's find Mommy and Daddy."

He babbled softly in my arms as we walked, knocking on doors, asking neighbors if they recognized him. No one did. We kept moving toward the church, hoping someone there would know. Families shook their heads, saying they'd never seen him before. My panic grew—until a little girl, maybe five years old, tugged at her mother's sleeve. Her mother had already said no, but the girl turned to us and said, "Oh, I know. Follow me."

She led us deeper into the church grounds, down into the basement—three flights of cement stairs, the air heavy with the smell of old stone and damp walls. At the bottom, she pointed to a family. In front of them sat an empty carrier.

I approached, clutching the boy. "Is he yours?" I asked.

The woman looked up, nodded casually, and said, "Yes, thanks," before turning away as if nothing had happened.

I couldn't hold back. My voice rose, echoing in the church basement. "Do you understand he was in the middle of the road, blocks down, about to get hit by a car? Pay attention next time!" My anger burned, but I swallowed it, remembering where I was. I walked out with Matthew, still shaking.

I knew we had saved that boy that day. My intuition hadn't let me down—the longer way had led us straight to him. A baby, alone, with no adult in sight, nearly falling into the street. Yes, we saved him.

And not long before that, another prayer had been answered. My cat, who had gone missing, was found in the middle of the woods. I had begged God to bring her back, and He did. That moment felt like a miracle, proof that sometimes what is lost can be found again.

But the miracle of finding my cat, and the intuition that saved the church boy, stood in painful contrast to what was coming next.

The rest of the day went well, but I could feel something unsettled in Matthew. He was annoyed, though he didn't say it outright. Maybe it was because I had been right, because my instincts had led us to that moment. Maybe it was because I bragged afterward, calling it magical, proud of what we had done. Or maybe it was because I couldn't stop fuming at those parents—how could they let their two-year-old slip away for so long without noticing?

That whole week, although everything seemed normal on

the surface, I felt the distance between us. Like he was hiding something. Briana was still giving me a hard time at work, and Matthew had been distancing himself there too, pretending to be busy, avoiding me. Everything felt off.

A few more days passed and it all came to a head. On the surface, it looked like any ordinary day — work, Ella's therapy appointment, Alfonzo's soccer practice. The only change was that soccer had been canceled because of the rain. Still, Matthew took Alfonzo across the street from Ella's therapist to toss a ball around, ignoring the light showers that fell. It wasn't until we got home later when everything shifted.

Matthew and I were in my vehicle when he asked me what was wrong. I told him I felt off — like he was hiding something from me. He had been acting strangely for the past week.

When I asked if he had been in contact with another female, he denied it and handed me his phone. As I scrolled, I found the texts with Briana. One message accused me of spreading a rumor about her and Matthew being involved. His response to her was, *"this has been addressed,"* though he had never mentioned anything to me. When I pressed him, he kept saying he didn't know. Further down, I saw messages that read *"come to queen"* and another that said *"in your bed **."* When I asked him to explain, he went silent, then muttered, *"let me explain — it wasn't her, it was this other girl, Queen."*

I told him it didn't matter who it was — everything he had told me in our relationship felt like a lie. I said I was done with the conversation.

Matthew refused to let it end. He said "no" and called his friend. I got out of the car, walking toward my house, but he followed me inside. Something felt wrong, so I turned back outside. He followed me again. I got into my car and closed the door, but he opened it, pushed me down into the front seat floor, and held me in a cradle-like position while still on the phone with his friend. He screamed, *"tell her who it was, tell her who it was,"* referring to me. His friend, confused, said, *"the time matches up, yeah that's your girl,"* not realizing it wasn't me.

Matthew had his hand around my neck, nearly sitting on me, holding me down while I remained pinned to the floor of the passenger seat. I was terrified. My mind raced: *What if he doesn't stop? What if he kills me right here? What if my children lose me tonight?*

Eventually, he let go and exited the vehicle. Moments later, he returned, threw my phone from my hand, grabbed me by the neck again, and said, *"Go ahead, tell them. You know what, I'm done. Go tell the neighbor, go tell Miguel, go be with them."*

He tried to go back inside my home, where my children were, but the front doors were locked. I searched frantically for my phone and keys to get inside and away from him. He threw my phone in the midst of calling his friend and pinning me down. Unable to find the phone, I grabbed the keys and ran toward the unlocked back door. Realizing he was chasing me, I diverted toward the side of the house, opened the gate, and he tackled me, throwing me down onto a rock before dragging me inside. Bruises were already forming on my arms, swelling from the impact. I was begging for him to stop.

Once inside, he began gathering his belongings, moving with a cold determination as if nothing had just happened. I stood there crying, my voice shaking as I told him he had hurt me. He looked at me without remorse and said flatly, *"You did this to yourself."*

My daughter, terrified, reached for the phone to call 911, but he snatched control of the situation. He dialed instead, claiming he was doing it to keep things from escalating. When he hung up, his tone shifted, darker, more threatening. *"Now let me give them a reason,"* he said.

He lunged toward me, wrapping both hands tightly around my neck. For several seconds, I couldn't breathe — my airway cut off, my body frozen in panic. Just as suddenly, he released his grip, leaving me gasping for air, my throat burning. Then, with chilling casualness, he tapped me on the nose, almost mockingly, and whispered his final threat: *"I'll be coming back for you, for Miguel, and for your precious neighbor."* When the police arrived, I said nothing. I was frozen, broken, terrified of what he would do if I spoke. My neck throbbed, swelling from his grip. I couldn't talk for two days afterward because of the damage.

My silence was its own prison. But after Matthew left that night, I called them back. Only then did I tell the truth of what had happened. It was honestly the hardest call I've ever made, but I knew I had to. For me. For my children. For the safety we deserved.

Still, the fear lingered. I was terrified he would return, that he would kill me, that he would hurt the kids. Every sound outside made me jump. Every shadow felt like him coming back. I couldn't shake the feeling that we were all marked, that he could appear at any moment.

So I gathered them and went to my neighbor's house. I slept there, not because I wanted to, but because I needed to feel like someone else was close by, someone who could help if he came back. I barely slept, lying awake, listening, waiting, watching cars pass on my cameras outside, praying the night would pass without him returning.

The next day, I went to my mother's. I couldn't be alone. I couldn't face the silence of my own house, the place where it had all happened. I just wanted to keep the kids safe, to surround them with family, to make sure they weren't left vulnerable.

But even there, the fear followed me. I kept replaying the night in my head — his hand around my neck, the way he dragged me inside, the threats he made. My body carried the evidence: bruises swelling on my arms from when he threw me to the ground, my neck so tender and swollen that I couldn't speak. Every time I tried to swallow or whisper, pain reminded me of what he had done.

I couldn't stop crying. Even when I wanted to, even when I tried to hold it in for the kids, the tears came anyway. I kept asking myself, *Why did this happen? How could the man I loved, the man I trusted, the man I let into my children's lives, do this to me?*

The kids saw me broken. They saw me scared. They saw me crying uncontrollably, my voice gone, my body marked. That's not something any child should ever have to witness. I could see the confusion in their eyes, the fear in their silence. They didn't know what to say, and I didn't know how to reassure them. How do you tell your children they're safe when you don't feel safe yourself?

And in the middle of all that fear, I again thought of my cat. Finding her that day had felt like a miracle, a reminder that sometimes prayers are answered, that sometimes what is lost can be found again.

But now, standing in my mother's house, bruised and broken, I wondered why my prayers hadn't been answered that night. Why had the man I loved turned into someone who terrified me? Why had my children been forced to see me like that? Why had Ella had to see it? The contrast was unbearable — the joy of finding my cat alive in the woods, and the devastation of losing all the trust I had in Matthew.

We were shattered — every one of us. My children carried the unbearable weight of what they had witnessed, and I carried the weight of what I had survived. The house no longer felt like a home; it had become a place of haunting memories, a crime scene where love had twisted into violence and trust had been destroyed.

That night, when the police finally understood what had happened, they pressed three charges against him: **strangulation, assault on a household member, and intimidation of a witness.** He was arrested shortly after the incident, but released on bond. To this day, I am still waiting for him to go to court and be formally charged.

The judge issued a no-contact order, but it was laughable — a mere two yards. Six feet apart. What does that even do? How does that protect me, or my children? They added special restrictions, but still allowed him to work. And because he was permitted to remain on site, to me, it meant I couldn't. How could I return to the same workplace knowing he was there? How could I face him in person after what he had done?

Even the thought of him was enough to unravel me. I couldn't imagine walking through those doors, pretending everything was normal, while carrying the trauma of that night. The fear was overwhelming, and the weight of everything pressed down on me — the bruises on my body, the silence of my children, the betrayal of the man I loved, the emptiness of my home. I felt broken in ways I didn't know how to repair.

I knew I couldn't go back — not yet, not like this. The pain was too raw, the fear too consuming. That realization marked the beginning of another chapter in my life: I had to step away from work, seek help, and face the truth that healing has no timeline.

I am still fractured, still clawing my way through the wreckage. Parts of me still love him — not the man who hurt me, but the version I built in my head. The version I saw a future with, a forever with. There's no way all those nights together, all the adventure, the passion, the sex, the coffee, the tea meant nothing. My heart knows that damaged people can cause damage to others. His childhood was broken, twisted. Some people are shaped by it; some let it define them.

I know what it feels like to be hurt. Some men carry their fathers' worst traits — they grow up watching their mothers get cheated on, beaten, and stay. They think it's normal. They know nothing else. And I know, as fucked up as it sounds, I still have love for him. I believe people can change if they want to. They can — but it takes dedication, it takes work, it takes a will stronger than the ghosts of the past. For now, I have to turn my will inward. I have to focus on me, and on my children. This is where my healing begins.

Shortly after Matthew was arrested, it wasn't long before DCF came crashing into my life. They rummaged through my home, spoke to my kids, their teachers, other parents, therapists, doctors — invading every corner of my privacy. Although the allegations made after the assault were completely false fabricated from shadows and spite, and ultimately determined to be unfounded by DCF, they still came in and somehow damaged me more. It was another wound, another violation, another reminder that survival is never simple.

This time away has reminded me of all the scars I carry — not just from him, but from everyone who has ever hurt me. I realized I needed to learn how to forgive. Not only him, but all of them. Every wound, every betrayal, every shadow from my past. I needed to air it out, in order to let it go, to stop letting those scars define me. Forgiveness doesn't mean forgetting. It means freeing myself from the weight of what was done to me, so I can finally breathe again.

One day, I may be healed from the trauma of my past. But today, I am still a mother, determined to build a life free from the toxic weight of my family's history so my children never have to carry it. I am still the daughter of a family that tried to break me. I am still an employee, holding onto hope that when this leave is over, I can return and move forward. I am still the girlfriend, still healing, who almost lost her life to the man she thought she would spend forever with. And though I am far from perfect, I know that right now, I am enough.

These are my subtle reflections — the quiet truths I whisper to myself when the world feels too heavy, the scars I acknowledge, the lessons I cannot ignore. They are the pieces of me I am piecing back together, the fragments of pain I am learning to release, and the beginnings of a healing that is mine alone to claim.

Forgiveness is the mirror I hold up to my scars, so I can finally see the strength beneath them.